An Crann Faoi Bhláth
The Flowering Tree

Declan Kiberd lectures in English at University College Dublin. His
published works include *Synge and the Irish Language* (second ed.,
1993), *Men and Feminism in Modern Literature*, *The Student's Annotated
Ulysses* (Penguin) and *Idir dhá Chultúr* (Coiscéim, 1993).

Gabriel Fitzmaurice is a National School Teacher in Moyvane, Co.
Kerry. Among his books are collections of poetry, anthologies and
children's verse in English and Irish and collections of songs and
ballads. His Irish language collections are *Nocht* (Coiscéim, 1989)
and *Nach Iontach Mar Atá* (Cló Iar Chonnachta, 1994). He is the editor
of *Irish Poetry Now: Other Voices* (Wolfhound Press, 1993).

An Crann Faoi Bhláth
The Flowering Tree

Contemporary Irish Poetry
with
Verse
Translations

Editors
Declan Kiberd

Gabriel Fitzmaurice

WOLFHOUND PRESS

The publisher receives financial assistance from The Arts Council/An Chomhairle Ealaíon, Ireland.

The co-operation of Bord na Gaeilge is acknowledged and appreciated by the publishers.

Reprinted 1995.
First published 1991 by
WOLFHOUND PRESS
68 Mountjoy Square, Dublin 1.

British Library Cataloguing in Publication Data
An crann faoi bhlath — The flowering tree.
    I. Title II. Kiberd, Declan III. Fitzmaurice, Gabriel IV. The flowering tree
    891 621408

    ISBN 0 86327 232 0 pb

Cover design: Jan de Fouw.
Cover illustration: detail from 'Wisteria and Other Blossoms Outside an Open Window at Kilkenny' by Mildred Anne Butler. Courtesy of Jim and Kay Canning.
Printed by Betaprint Ltd

Contents

Acknowledgements

For permission to reprint poems in this anthology, we would like to acknowledge the following with thanks, For poems by: Colm Breathnach, the author. Deaglán Collinge from *Sealgaireacht*, An Clóchomhar. Michael Davitt from *Bligeard Sráide*, Coiscéim; and for 'Poker' from *Ghleann ar Ghleann*, Sáirséal Ó Marcaigh. Conleth Ellis from *Fómhar na nGeanna*, Clódhanna Teoranta; and from *Seabhac ag Guairdeall*, Coiscéim. Pearse Hutchinson from *Faoistin Bhacach*, An Clóchomhar. Biddy Jenkinson from *Báisteach Gintlí*, Coiscéim. Pádraig Mac Fhearghusa from *Faoi Léigear*, An Clóchomhar; and for lines from *Notaí Treallchogaíochta Ó 'Suburbia*, Clódhanna Teoranta. Tomás Mac Síomóin from *Codarsnaí*, Clódhanna Teoranta. Caitlín Maude from *Dánta*, Coiscéim. Máire Mhac an tSaoi from *Margadh na Saoire, Codladh an Ghaiscígh agus Véarsaí Eile* and *An Galar Dubhach*, Sáirséal Ó Marcaigh. Nuala Ní Dhomhnaill from *Fearr Suaithinseach*, An Sagairt; and for 'Póg' from *An Dealg Droighin*, Mercier Press. Áine Ní Ghlinn from *An Chéim Bhriste*, Coiscéim. Mícheál Ó hAirtnéide from *Adharca Broic*; and lines from *An Phurgóid*, Gallery Press; Breandán Ó Beacháin from *Poems and a Play in Irish*, Gallery Press. Máirtín Ó Direáin from *Coinnle Geala, Dánta Eile* and *Dánta Aniar*, Sáirséal Ó Marcaigh; and from *Ár Ré Dhearóil*, Goldsmith Press. Seán Ó hÉigeartaigh from *Cama-Shiúlta*, An Clóchomhar. Art Ó Maolfabhail from *Aistí Dánta*, Sáirséal Ó Marcaigh. Aogán Ó Muircheartaigh from *Oíche Gréine*, Coiscéim. Liam Ó Muirthile from *Tine Chnámh*, Sáirséal Ó Marcaigh. Muiris Ó Ríordáin, the author. Seán Ó Ríordáin from *Eireaball Spideoige* and *Línte Limbo*, Sáirséal Ó Marcaigh. Cathal Ó Searcaigh from *Súile Shuibhne*, Coiscéim. Mícheál Ó Siadhail from *Runga, Cumann* and *An Bhlian Bhiagh*, An Clóchomhar. Eoghan Ó Tuairisc from *Dialann Sa Díseart*, Coiscéim; and from *Lux Aeterna*, Rita Kelly. Seán Ó Tuama for 'Besides, Who Knows Before The End, What Light May Shine', the author; and from *Saol Fo Thoinn*, An Clóchomhar. Gabriel Rosenstock from *Óm* and *Migmas*, An Clóchomhar. Eithne Strong from *Sarah in Passing*, the author. Tomás Tóibín from *Dulliúr*, Coiscéim; and from *Súil Le Cuan*, Cló Morainn.

For translations as credited in the text, we acknowledge the following with thanks: Greg Delanty, Conleth Ellis, Gabriel Fitzmaurice, Michael Hartnett, Pádraig Mac Fhearghusa, Tomás Mac Síomóin, David Marcus, Paul Muldoon, Ulick O'Connor, Muiris Ó Ríordáin, Pádraigín Riggs, Douglas Sealy, and the authors.

Introduction

DECLAN KIBERD

It has been said more than once that a writer's duty is to
insult, rather than flatter. Yeats inclined to the view that
whenever a country produced a man of genius, he was
never like that country's idea of itself. Without a doubt,
the literary movement now known as modernism con-
sisted primarily in a revolt against all prevalent styles
and a rebellion against official order; and yet, by its very
innovative nature, it was precluded from establishing a
fixed style of its own. 'Modernism must struggle but
never triumph', observed Irving Howe, 'and in the end
must struggle in order *not* to triumph'.

By the 1960s, this movement had come to an end, as
society tamed and domesticated its wild bohemians,
converting them from radical dissidents into slick enter-
tainments. 'The avant-garde writer', bemoaned Howe,
'must confront the one challenge for which he has not
been prepared: the challenge of success . . . Meanwhile,
the decor of yesterday is appropriated and slicked up;
the noise of revolt magnified in a frolic of emptiness; and
what little remains of modernism denied so much as the
dignity of an opposition'.

Irish modernism had been largely an emigrant's af-
fair—and those Gaelic writers who remained at home
produced not a literature which peered into the abyss or
fought the new establishment, but one which (in the view
of Máirtín Ó Cadhain) was more suited to an audience of
credulous schoolchildren and preconciliar nuns. In his
novel *Cré na Cille* (1949) Ó Cadhain produced the one
undisputed masterpiece of Gaelic Modernism. If Beckett

had to cope with a language of exhaustion, then in that book Ó Cadhain offered a response to the exhaustion of a language. There were many who believed that Ó Cadhain's graveyard, with its talking corpses, was the epitome of the state to which the Irish language had fallen in the mid-century. Among politicians, the argument seemed no longer about ways of saving the language, but rather about who had responsibility for the corpse. But, in the words of Nóra Sheáinín, the fey philosopher of that narrative, *ars longa, vita brevis*, Ó Cadhain was already shoring against his ruins, looking forward to a time when his book would survive even the death of the language in which it was written. The book's central location in a graveyard is not a metaphor of the fate of Irish, but of the fate of itself. Ó Cadhain shared with Beckett the secret knowledge that even when language dies, the voices continue:

> All the dead voices.
> They make a noise like wings . . .
> To have lived is not enough for them.
> They have to talk about it.

Unlike Beckett, however, Ó Cadhain did not have to seek out debility, self-impoverishment, and estrangement. The culture in which he functioned was estranged from the start.

It was this apparent weakness of the Irish language which became the saving of its literature. If modernism is a literature of extreme situations, then few groups have professed this sense of extremity more obviously than the Irish—Synge's Aran peasants live on the outermost edges of Europe; Tomás Ó Criomhthain reminds us that the next parish is America; and Muiris Ó Súilleabháin goes so far as to say that he is not an Irishman but a Blasketman (rather like Flaubert who claimed Bohemia, and not France, as his native country). By the 1960s, however, Irish modernism was at a virtual end. Having lived for decades on the edge of things, at limits where other lungs would have found the air unbreathable, writers of English were encouraged to return to the homeland and claim their share in the new riches. The government, which had banned most good writing in English over the previous decades, announced a tax-holiday for creative artists.

Even in the bad old days, the standing army of Irish poets had never fallen below five thousand (as Patrick Kavanagh jibed), but now that number swelled with every passing week. Writers—as opposed to writing—had become big business. Some government ministers even appeared in photographs alongside authors whose work had been recently banned. These artists embodied for the new Irish bourgeoisie all those qualities which decades of money-grubbing had led the Paudeens to reject in themselves, lyricism, prodigality, spirituality and open-heartedness. The results were predictable. As Howe foretold, bracing enmity gave way to wet embraces. Many second-rate figures appeared to enact in public the role of writer, rather than confront in private the anguish of real writing. By the end of the 1970s, the Fianna Fáil government instituted the *aos dána*, a group of about 150 artists who would be paid an annual stipend and accorded state homage. Cynics remarked that this honeymoon between politician and artist might end when the *aos* became truly *dána* and emulated the cantankerous behaviour of ancient bards dissatisfied with the behaviour of a chief. But the *aos dána* proved as tame as they were grateful.

The position of writers in Irish during the 1960s was

somewhat different. For decades, they had been en-
gaged in a protracted honeymoon with the government
and state agencies; but the marriage had proved less then
fruitful. The massive attempts to revive and spread the
Irish language, at the beginning of the century, had been
attended by no great revival of Gaelic writing. Indeed,
writers of English had seemed to draw the last drops of
blood from the expiring body, and to inject those toxins
into their own offspring to invigorating effect. Anglo-
Irish literature fed like a parasite off its dying parent; and
yet the more extensive the efforts at reviving Irish, the
poorer the quality of the literature actually produced.

By the 1970s, when the official pretence of revival was
less and less convincing, and when a passing mark in the
language was no longer compulsory in state examina-
tions, the literature of Irish enjoyed a minor renaissance.
Much of this energy was due to the inspiration of Máirtín
Ó Cadhain, by 1970 at the end of a great career as
Professor of Irish at Trinity College Dublin; and much of
the zest came from the skill with which men like
Desmond Fennell presented the language movement as
part of the counter-culture—a return to healthy rural
values, to peripheries rather then centres, to civil rights
for small communities rather than national emblems for
large, impersonal bureaucracies. While the youth of
America marched with black leaders on the Pentagon
and while Bernadette Devlin (herself a student of Irish at
university) marched for democracy on Stormont Castle
in Belfast, men like Ó Cadhain and Fennell marched
through Connemara in a movement that would lead to a
devolved government, local radio stations and, by no
coincidence, a revival of Gaelic poetry.

And this, too, was grounded in a paradox, for the
youthful poets who supported Cearta Sibhialta na Gael-

tachta in 1969 would make their subsequent careers not in the Gaeltacht, but in large cities from which most of them anyway came. And they would renew not the prose tradition so beloved of Ó Cadhain, but the poetic forms for most of which he had such ill-disguised scorn. In the last major lecture, delivered just a year before his death, *Páipéir Bhána agus Páipéir Bhreaca*, Ó Cadhain mocked the very movement which he, more than any other, had helped to create:

> Staid bhagarach, drochthuar é, an iomarca tóir a bheith ar fhilíocht a chuma le hais an phróis. Seo mar tá sé i mionteangachaí eile ar nós Gáidhlig na hAlban, a bhfuil triúr nó ceathrar filí den scoth inti freisin . . . Na cúpla file maith atá againn, níl siad ag cuma a ndóthain. Is fusa go fada liric dheas ne-amhurchóideach ocht líne a chuma anois agus aríst ná aiste a scríobh, urscéal, ná fiú gearrscéal féin a scríobh. Seo í an éascaíocht agus an leisce ar ais aríst. Chó fada is is léar dhomsa is mó go mór a bhfuil d'fhilíocht dhá scríobh sa nGaeilge ná sa mBéarla in Éirinn . . . Sé an prós tathán coincréad, clocha saoirsinne an tsaoil, agus é chó garbh, míth-aitneamhach leis an saol féin. Sileadh gur gaile-maisíocht a bhí ar Phatrick Kavanagh nuair adeireadh sé gurbh fhileata go mór iad na prós-scribhneoirí, daoine mar O'Flaherty nó O'Connor, ná na filí Gall-Ghaelacha. Le galra seo na filíocht a bhí sé ag plé . . . Is beag atá fághta ag an bhfilíocht inniu. Níl tada fághta aici sa nGaeilge ach liricí gearra . . .

It is a threatening and ominous portent when there is an excessive zeal to compose poetry rather than prose. This is also the situation in other minority languages, including Scots Gaelic, which has three or four first-rate poets working in the language as well . . . The few good poets of our own are not composing a sufficient amount. It is easier by far to write a nice, harmless eight-line lyric now and again than to write an essay, a novel, or even a short story. This heralds a return to glib facility and laziness. As far as I can make out, far more poetry is being written in Irish than in English here in Ireland. Prose is the concrete base, the mason's cornerstone of life; and it is as rough and unpleasant as life itself. It was thought that Patrick Kavanagh engaged in special pleading when he said that prose writers such as O'Flaherty and O'Connor were much more poetic than the Anglo-Irish poets. He was referring to the disease of poetry . . . These days there is little left for poetry to do. Nothing is left to poetry in Irish but brief lyrics . . .

Ó Cadhain asserted that nothing should be written in the lyric form which could not be equally well said in prose (hardly a revolutionary demand); but he seemed to imply the superior range and versatility of prose when he skilfully deployed the criticism of Edmund Wilson to make his point for him: 'The technique of prose today seems thus to be absorbing the technique of verse; but it is showing itself equal to the work'.

At the time of its delivery, this lecture was construed as a frontal assault on poetry (and Seán Ó Ríordáin responded accordingly); but also as a covert critique of the woolly-mindedness of the young. The University College Cork poets associated with *Innti* magazine through the 1970s—Davitt, Rosenstock, Ó Muirthile and Ní Dhomhnaill—had to bear the burden of this formidable disapproval; but bear it they did, remaining steadfast in their defence of the Gaelic lyric, which they infused with the cultural deposits of the 1960s, from Zen Buddhism to Dylanesque symbology.

The death of Ó Cadhain in 1970 saw the proseman raised to canonical status and made the task of the younger poets, if anything, more difficult. They were helped from the beginning by enthusiastic and large audiences among their own generation. For the first time ever, writing in Irish was addressed not to the Gaelic race (whatever that might be), but to specific groups, illustrating Scott Fitzgerald's dictum that an artist writes for the youth of today, the critics of tomorrow and the schoolmasters of ever afterward. The rate of social change in Ireland was such that the old seemed to occupy a time-warp of their own; and though an occasional young poet might write a lyric of homage to an established master, such as Davitt's to Ó Direáin, astute readers often found that the laconic recreation of the senior lyricist's modes skirted the edge of insolent parody. Of course, nobody would know better than Máirtín Ó Direáin, the leading survivor of the older generation, just how essential such insolence is to a living tradition. Ó Direáin might not catch all the counter-cultural resonances of *Positively Sráid Fhearchair*, but he had read and well understood *Tradition and the Individual Talent*. The war on the past took many forms, but, in a case such as this, an insulting imitation was the sincerest form of flattery.

Poets like Davitt, Rosenstock and Ní Dhomhnaill spoke for, as well as to, a wide audience, most of whose members were urban, middle-class and radical, unlike the previous generation of authors who tended to hail from the Gaeltacht or semi-Gaeltacht, and to be rural, impoverished, and conservative in ideology. Instead of pandering to the placid, already-converted audience of senior Irish-speaking citizens, the *Innti* poets went out and created a largely new audience for poetry. Not only that, but the interviews and essays published in their journal helped to create the taste by which they would eventually be judged. At the height of this revival, it was widely believed that there were more readers in Ireland for a poem written in Irish than for one in English, though whether all these enthusiasts applied aesthetic (rather than nationalistic) criteria is debatable. It is, of course, the peculiar destiny of innovators to seem less and less remarkable in proportion to their success in changing public taste; and if, by the 1980s, both *Innti* and its poets were attracting smaller audiences they could at least console themselves with the knowledge that the senior critical figures in universities had finally admitted their work as a valid and valuable extension of the Gaelic canon. In December 1984, writing in *Comhar*, Eoghan Ó Hanluain gave *Innti* a clean bill of academic health. It is, perhaps, a measure of the growing conservatism of the *Innti* poets that some pronounced themselves grateful and pleased.

Had Máirtín Ó Cadhain lived for another decade, he might have wished to rephrase, if not reverse, his judgements. The war which he proclaimed was phoney from the outset, for if Ó Cadhain could write poetry in prose, then it was also possible for Áine Ní Ghlinn to flirt with the possibility of a kind of prose in verse. The very Kavanagh whom Ó Cadhain had invoked in his attack on the young poets had himself proclaimed that it was his lifelong ambition 'to play a true note on a dead slack string', to deflate the modernist intensity of a Yeats with the ad-lib techniques of 'Not-caring':

No one will speak in prose
Who finds his way to those Parnassian
  Islands . . .
—but he will do the next best thing!
The notion that the distinction between poetry and prose
is a typographical conceit is part of a much wider post-
modern attempt to annul all polarities. The poets in this
volume, or at least the younger among them, ask us to
unlearn the illusory differences between men and
women, reason and emotion, Irish and English.

The premier literary journal of the period *Scríobh* re-
cognised no division between creative and critical writ-
ing, opening its pages to the academic specialist and the
working artist alike; while, at the same time, poets incor-
porated elements of auto-criticism into their creative
texts. This may have been motivated by the desire to
render these texts invulnerable to academic exegesis, by
beating the scholar to the critical punch, for, from its
beginnings, Gaelic poetry, though practised by persons
of wit and erudition, has shown a healthy disrespect for
pedantry. As Séan Ó Ríordáin wrote of his poems;

Má chastar libh fear léinn sa tslí,
Bhur rún ná ligidh leis, bhur mian,—
ní dá leithéid a cumadh sibh . . .

If you meet a learned man on the way
Do not let slip to him your secret, your desire
It wasn't for his sort that you were made

But it was also, and more probably, part of the in-
ternational attempt by poets to create a wholly self-
sufficient work of art, containing within itself its own
critical apparatus.

What all this proved was simple enough—that the
best literature is an act of consummate criticism, and the

best criticism is literature in the profoundest sense. In the great works of this century, the two became indistinguishable, as the French novelist Alain Robbe-Grillet observed:

> It seems as though we are making our way more and more towards an epoch in fiction in which the problems of writing will be seen clearly by the novelist, and in which critical concerns, far from sterilising creation, will be able on the contrary to serve it as a motive force.

The inevitable consequence is that, as criticism grows more academic and solemn, literature is increasingly learning to laugh at itself. Though many of the poems in this volume are, predictably, about the process of making poetry, all but a few are written with a degree of irony and self-effacement. Like Kavanagh—a significant source for poets in Irish as well as English—these artists are happy to treat literature as a mere aspect of life, rather than a high road to salvation. By reducing the extravagant claims made by Yeats for poetry, they manage to lodge the reasserted, but more modest, claim with a fair degree of conviction. The poems, as a result, are not irritatingly self-conscious, but healthily self-aware; and the learning, quite impressive in some cases, is lightly carried. At a time when Irish poetry in English grows more heavily allusive each year—as if the text were created in, and not just written for, the university seminar—this poetry was blessedly free of Danteesque echoes or mythical claptrap. Indeed, so resolutely anti-academic had it been in its earlier phases, that the educational establishment responded in kind by keeping many of the younger poets off school-courses.

*   *   *   *   *   *   *

If the Gaelic tradition offered a life-support mechanism for Yeats, Synge and the many Anglo-Irish contemporaries during the period of national revival, then the reverse has been the case in recent decades, as Gaelic poets turn for inspiration to the work of these figures. There has, indeed, been a real *rapprochement* between the two traditions; and this is clear also in the number of translations from Gaelic to English performed by a range of leading poets from Heaney to Kinsella. Even more crucial to this closening of ties has been the sheer number of artists producing high-quality work in both languages—Brendan Behan, Pearse Hutchinson, Críostóir Ó Floinn, Michael Hartnett and Mícheál Ó Siadhail are simply the latest exponents of a great tradition of bilingualism that reaches back , *via* Flann O'Brien and Liam O'Flaherty, to Patrick Pearse.

The phrase *ag obair as lámha a chéile* (working out of one another's hands) might well characterise the current relationship between writers of English and Irish. Paul Muldoon's translation of Davitt's *An Scáthán* is probably as well known as its brilliant original; while Mícheál Ó Siadhail's English versions of his own lyrics have achieved a reputation in their own right. The deference shown to Yeats, especially by the young, is remarkable. Mícheál Ó Siadhail's compliment to the women in his life

Two or three drew the thread together
And wove for me a shirt . . .

though nicely ironical in its image of shirt as shroud, is clearly indebted to Yeats's

Three women who have wrought
What joy is in my days . . .

as, indeed, to Kavanagh's 'God in Woman'. The cultivation of an italicised balladic refrain is another Yeatsian ploy favoured by many, while Ó Direáin's characteristic imagery of tree, stone and wave-whitened bone has its acknowledged source in Yeats.

In a somewhat similar fashion, the use of sacred imagery to brashly profane purpose, which was a feature of Synge's art, may be found in poets as varied as Ó Searcaigh

On the altar of the bed,
I celebrate your body tonight, my love . . .

and Mac Fhearghusa

Give us a hint, God,
What kind of place is Heaven?
According to what I hear
The place isn't greatly to my liking . . .

This is in keeping with the Gaelic proverb which says that God possesses the heavens but covets the earth; and also with Christy Mahon's pity, as he squeezes kisses on his lover's lips, for the Lord God sitting lonesome in his golden chair.

The homages to Yeats and his Anglo-Irish contemporaries may spring from a deep-felt desire to fuse the two island traditions in a single work of literature as an emblem of Irish possibility, but such homage is all the more remarkable in view of the fact that contemporary Irish poetry in English is increasingly identifying its true parent as Joyce. Dillon Johnston's *Irish Poetry After Joyce* (1985) was just the first of what will doubtless be a succession of books written to substantiate that claim. Hence, our paradox—that while Ó Direáin was penning heartfelt tributes to Yeats in *Comhar*, Kavanagh was pouring scorn on the man whom he saw as the last of the

Eminent Victorians:

> Yes, Yeats, it was damn easy for you, protected
> By the middle classes and the Big Houses,
> To talk about the sixty-year-old public
>   protected
> Man, sheltered by the dim Victorian muses.

What attracted Kavanagh to Joyce was his rediscovery of the mythical in the matter-of-fact, his evocation of the wanderings of Odysseus in the voyage through Dublin of a nondescript canvasser of ads. Kavanagh's *Epic*, in sonnet form, casts a small-town quarrel over the owner-ship of fields against a similar backdrop:

> That was the year of the Munich bother. Which
> Was more important? I inclined
> To lose my faith in Ballyrush and Gortin
> Till Homer's ghost came whispering to my
>   mind.
> He said: I made the Illiad from such
> A local row. Gods make their own importance.

While, at first glance, it might seem as if the ancient epic is invoked to belittle the struggles of latter-day pygmies, in the end it is clear that the banal concerns of everyday men are used to question the notion of ancient heroism.

This was not exactly the understanding on which Yeats's poetry was based, which is, of course, why Joyce steered clear of the warlike Cúchulain and chose instead as his model the homely and draft-dodging Odysseus. Seamus Heaney's poem *The Tollund Man* bases itself on a comparable strategy. Here, the sacrifical victim of an ancient fertility rite is dug out of the Danish bog, his body preserved down even to his half-digested seedcake, to recall for us the banality of ancient as well as contempo-

rary evil. Heaney says he could consecrate the bog as
holy ground, install the Tollund Man as a pagan god

<blockquote>

and pray
Him to make germinate

The scattered, ambushed
Flesh of labourers,
Stockinged corpses
Laid out in the farmyards.
</blockquote>

Pádraig MacFhearghusa uses the figure of Neandertha-
lus in identical fashion, addressing him in his grave
beneath the Zagros mountains:

<blockquote>
Moistly may the pollen grains
of your body
fecundate us,
That we may lay aside
at the mouth of your grave
the scorched briars
of shiftless power,
That from our eye
may fall
a black fertile tear
on the grey ashes
of our tribes consumed . . .
</blockquote>

The elevation of Joyce to a position of primacy in the
story of modern Irish poetry is another illustration of Ó
Cadhain's contention that prose could now take on most
of the tasks traditionally assigned to verse. The conse-
quent diminution of Yeats is not without its cruel ironies,
for the 'Joycean' commingling of the mythical and the
material had its actual roots in the Yeatsian theatre.
'What we wanted', said Lady Gregory of the Abbey

Theatre, 'was to create for Ireland a theatre with a base of realism and an apex of beauty'—or, as Lennox Robinson later phrased it, a reconciliation of 'poetry of speech' with 'humdrum facts'. Yeats himself endorses the method in his play *On Baile's Strand* where the irrelevance of Cúchulain's poetic posturing to the needs of the proletarians in the prosaic sub-plot is the drama's underlying theme.

Wherever we look in the contemporary zones of Gaelic poetry, we may come upon this interrogation of the mythical by the matter-of-fact. This works, most often, in terms of the humiliation of tradition by the individual talent, the denial of national myths in the face of authentic personal feeling. The self is the new touchstone; and so the source of ethical judgements changes. The impact on the self, and not the moral consequences for society, becomes the most popular yardstick for measuring an action. So, in *Spring Thaw*, Declan Collinge's lovers rekindle their flame against an ice-age backdrop; and even though the legendary giant of Kippure mountain starts to stir in his sleep, he seems strangely ancillary to the scene. Perhaps Mícheál Ó Siadhail pursues this strategy best. His *Stony Patch* is a complex reworking of the same theme, because he is as anxious to humanise the past as the present. If Joyce's ancient hero turns out on closer inspection to have been a draft-dodger, then Ó Siadhail is also aware that the remnants of a life are a mimicry rather than a full representation. What is left is the search for some sign of the persistence of the person, some hint of the complexities lost to the ravages of time. Our respect, hints Ó Siadhail, should be given to the matter-of-factness of the Egyptian hermits and Skellig monks, rather than to the *post-factum* myths of simplification—for, like Yeats's meditators on

Mount Meru, and like the modern artist, they too were self-invented men, each one 'scratching his song in the wax of his soul', or working 'in the tradition of himself'.

Ó Siadhail's *Nugent*, though superficially a very different type of poem, is an even more astute reworking of the same materials, for here the matter-of-fact is elevated to the status of the mythical. The first republican prisoner is released, after two years and three quarters on the blanket-protest, to become an instant newspaper celebrity, only to be diminished almost at once by his proximity to banal news of 'the last race from Naas'. The single photograph, a moment frozen in time, is all we moderns know of Nugent, and all he will finally be allowed to know of himself. It cruelly deprives the nationalist rebel of his own history, of the tradition of himself for 'what space has news or history?' The remainder of the poem becomes Ó Siadhail's attempt to reinsert this figure into his own narrative, with irony as well as love, since Nugent is a name not of Gaelic but of foreign origin. This republican may even be descended from those very Dutch mercenaries who invaded Ireland to found the Orange ascendancy which Nugent himself now fights. Cast in this European perspective, Nugent becomes a kind of universal soldier:

> But in the fear of Nugent's eye
> Walks the last private soldier,
> Famished, bedraggled after Napoleon;
> All camp followers who ever tramped,
> Smarting for our comfort,
> Across the cold land of history.
> Were those his own crazed eyes
> Who terrified us so?

Already, this still-born myth has been almost erased by

the matter-of-fact, for 'tomorrow the back-room must be put in order', and even now Nugent's photograph has been 'covered over/by a spatter of paint'.

The poem, though it lovingly celebrates this domestic ritual, seems nevertheless profoundly troubled by its elevation of the private over the public world. Though the poet repeats Daniel O'Connell's aphorism that the cause may not be worth a drop of blood, he has the artistic courage to leave the last word to Nugent and to that question which forms in the prisoner's eyes. As is the case in *Patient*, the pain in those eyes is but an aspect of the suffering of the poet, who looks into them with an acute awareness of other lives which the prisoner might have had. There is, however, nothing patronising about the sympathy offered in either poem. On the contrary, there is humility in the poet's admission that he cannot gaze on the unfathomable, but can merely 'by indirections find directions out' and look quizzically into the eyes of those who have the courage to peer into the unknown. Only he experiences a need to name and, therefore, to control—he itemises the nature of a patient's disease or the history of a surname—and that is his foremost duty as poet. He offers a private judgement of Nugent's wasted years, as they appear to him, but concedes the awesome integrity of the man's option, and tenderly restores to him that full history which the news photograph had threatened to abort.

Integrity, here, lies in the scrupulous balance kept between sympathy and condemnation. Where most poets would lapse into facile condemnations of violence, or (less likely) glib endorsements of Nugent's heroism, or (very common and worst of all) automatic attempts to steer some middle course of suspended judgements, Ó Siadhail has the courage to make his own views clear, while conceding that Nugent remains finally mysterious, ineffable, beyond the neat formulations of the local newspaper or, indeed, the home handyman's poem.

Something of a similar complexity is achieved by Michael Davitt in *For Bobby Sands on the Day before he Died*. This is a poem which perfectly captures the luxurious marginality of the south in the face of all northern suffering, and the fake intensity of its debate. Davitt is the gentlest of poets and there is a streak of sentimentality in the final prayer, which is an attempt to rewind the reel of history rather than play it through. Nevertheless, both this and *Nugent* are among the very few political poems written in Irish under the strain of the northern crisis which manage to be political and yet remain poems. Others have generally opted for the easier, and fashionable, strategy of calling down a plague on all public worlds and celebrating instead the intensities of the personal life. One is left with the impression that nationalism, perhaps because there was so much of it in the bad poetry of previous generations, is deemed radioactive — so much so that it cannot be condemned, or praised, or even mentioned at all. No poet of the *Innti* generation would echo the hopeful simplicities of Ó Direáin:

I dtír inar chuir filí tráth
Tine Cásca ar lasadh,
Ní lastar tinte cnámh
Ar árda do do shamhail . . .
Is abair nuair is caothúil
Gur dhí na céille an galar
A bhí ar na móir atá marbh
Anois nuair nach mairid
Ní heagal duit a nagairt.

In a land where poets once

Put Easter fires ablaze,
Bonfires are not lighted
On hilltops for your like . . .
And say when it is convenient
That stupidity was the illness
Which beset the great ones who are dead.
Now that they are no longer living,
You need not fear their challenge.

The irony is that these words were addressed to those younger poets, who, for the most part, have politely refused to be drawn into such debates.

For some younger writers, 'politics' is a debate not about hunger strikes and dirty protests, but atom bombs, US foreign policy and the cost of living. In *The Harlot's Secret* the most common poetic strategy of our time is followed by Declan Collinge, as the private resolution of a prostitute to live respectably on the money earned by her memoirs rocks the composure of bishop and politician. For this generation, all isms are wasms; and frequently it is only the labyrinth of sexual relations which can evoke a truly complex poem. National ideals, where they survive, can only be treated tangentially; and so Collinge's poem on the bald eagle in Philadelphia Zoo seems to discern in the decay of one republic the fate of another. Caitlín Maude's *Vietnam Love Song* is even more resolute in its avoidance of all public worlds:

the hawk hovering in the air
awaiting the stench of death

and in its, by now suspect, assurance that private havens may be found in an otherwise heartless world:

we could have stayed on the field of slaughter,
but the sad faces of the soldiers

made us laugh
and we chose a soft place by the river.

Rarely enough is there any recognition of the fact that the personal refuge may itself recapitulate all the distortions and wickedness of the outside world. Far more typical is Maude's option for the soft place by the river, in whose depths the unconscious may be plumbed, and by whose shores the self may be dramatised. Perhaps all this is predictable enough, for even an intensely political poet like Yeats, after his writings on the civil war, never again conceived of happiness in social rather than domestic terms.

It is only in the work of Seán Ó Ríordáin and Máirtín Ó Direáin—both, significantly of an older generation which started out in the 1940s—that there is any extensive attempt to chart the links between the private and public world. By another curious paradox, this is achieved by these most lonely and most private of men. Their poems are based on the notion that only the outsider-figure truly knows the values held by a community, whose members are always too busy living life to appraise, and therefore to possess, it. There is, says Ó Ríordáin, 'a local music/that its speakers do not hear'. As an isolate, Ó Ríordáin is filled with contempt for mass-culture, where freedom turns out to be the freedom to be like everybody else and true freedom is a bleakness which very few can endure. On the other hand, however, he envies the Gaeltacht community which he visits its apparently effortless achievement of communal value:

The love of my heart I'll give to people
to whom nothing has appeared
but other's thoughts.

But there is no final relief to be found in the Gaeltacht,

either. Like Synge, the poet feels himself a mere 'inter-loper'; and, anyway, the community is revealed as a degenerate fiction, a myth which has been exploded. The 'Gaelic community' is a zone for tourists, but not a recognisable place where anyone lives.

A remarkable number of poems in the volume do, indeed, take the form of spiritual tourism of one kind or another—Ó Ríordáin in Mount Mellery (anticipating Heaney's *Station Island* in tone and theme by decades), Ó Muirthile in Maoinis, Collinge in Philadelphia Zoo. The impression is given of the world—and especially Ireland—as a gigantic open-air museum, in which remnants of the past can be examined by a process of instant archaeology. The past, like art, exists as just another item to be consumed; and, since nothing is more remote than the recently abandoned past, nothing is treated with more ferocity.

The official pretence—that there was still a sizeable Irish-speaking community in the Gaeltacht—was ex-ploded by Desmond Fennell at the end of the 1970s; and he himself returned to a Dublin where most of the poets were already trying to gear Irish to a post-Gaeltacht, post-industrial, post-Christian, post-everything society. Davitt's jibe at the 'céad míle fáilte' (hundred thousand welcomes), offered to the incoming visitor by the Irish Tourist Board, took the form of a hundred and one farewells offered to the few post-inflationary visitors and departing emigrants; but such nose-thumbing could not conceal the fact that the Irish were virtual tourists in their own country now. The same material greed which priced Irish holidays out of the international market had served also to erase centuries-old traditions. Thatched cottages were abandoned to ruin, as hacienda bunga-lows rose up in their stead, with names like 'South Fork' and 'High Chapparal'. So rapid were the changes that the native Irish themselves began to take the place of absent foreign visitors, in an attempt to exhume on a fortnight's holiday their all-but-buried past. Tourist slogans which, a generation earlier, might have been beamed at a British or American audience, were now directed at the Irish themselves: 'Discover Ireland; it's part of what you are'. Significantly, the latter phrase had already been used in government promotional campaigns for the Irish language. Some city boys, like Ó Muirthile in Maoinis, or even Behan, in an earlier generation, on the Blaskets, were beguiled for a time by such pastoralism; but a majority endorsed the war against the past.

So, in *Entreaty*, Caitlín Maude implores her man not to impose any past pattern of Celtic lovers (Diarmaid and Gráinne) upon the present fact:

> do not speak,
> young man,
> my 'Diarmaid',
> and we will be at peace.

The rejection of 'literature' and of literary stances is a recurrent theme, along with the suspicion that there is corruption at the very heart of beauty. The latter, of course, is an ancient Gaelic notion, to be found in the legend of Deirdre, who threatened to destroy her beauty in order to thwart the besotted king who tried to kill her lover. Even more notable is an awareness of the past as a burden rather than an enrichment. Áine Ní Ghlinn's *Racial Pride* concedes that the cry of ancestors, though it may tear us apart, must be kept alive, and not because that cry is a sign of self-confidence but because the only alternative is a grey, dreary meaninglessness. Culture thus becomes a self-confessed tautology by which, in Eliot's terms, we rejoice in being able to construct something upon which to rejoice.

We fear to pay the full costs of our debt to the past—as we fear the steady gaze of Nugent—and yet we also desire to clear the bill once and for all, lest our refusal to do so constitute an allegation against ourselves as well as our ancestors. Not all, of course, are so tender towards the tradition. The continental poet Apollinaire once said that you can't lug the corpse of your father around on your back for the rest of your life; and so Davitt can call for a clean slate, creation *ex nihilo*:

> We will singe our barren bards
> in a bonfire
> and scatter their ashes
> on the mildew of tradition . . .

though it must be added that he is equally dismissive of Marxist notions of political determinism:

> We will bid farewell
> to the historic train
> that goes astray.

Creation out of nothing is, in the end, impossible and a Gaelic poet may burn his bards only to find himself reaching for the writings of Joyce, Keats, Wordsworth or whomever. Gaelic poetry has always enjoyed a living connection with European art, from the age of *amour courtois* to the versions of Catalan by Pearse Hutchinson; and that, in turn, has been complicated, as well as enhanced, by the growing American connection. If Seferis and the Greeks lie on the shelves of Seán Ó Tuama, or the love-poets of France on the mantelpiece of Máire Mhac an tSaoi, then John Berryman lies alongside the collections of local folklore which animate the muse of Nuala Ní Dhomhnaill. Pop-art and Bob Dylan may inform a lyric by Davitt or Collinge; Kavanagh and Bronislaw Malinowski may inspire Mícheál Ó Siadhail; Eliot's human voices may awaken Caitlín Maude to a whole series of American accents, the most detectable of which is Emily Dickinson's:

> the loss of
> Heaven
> is the worst Hell.

seems to echo

> Parting is all we know of Heaven
> And all we need of Hell.

There is a Keatsian ring to her 'sweeter still / is the word / that was never uttered'.

There can be no doubt, however, that the major influence is Joyce, most palpable in the work of Ó Ríordáin, far and away the leading poet of the period. Like Joyce's, his mind was saturated with the symbols of the Roman Catholicism which he had learned to reject; and, like Joyce, he put the repudiated terminology of theology to use in evolving a personal aesthetic theory. If Joyce spoke of 'epiphanies' as moments of sudden spiritual manifestation, Ó Ríordáin wrote of the 'beo-gheit' which leaves us sacramentally 'fé ghné eile' (under a different aspect). If Joyce annexed the Eucharist for his *epicleti*, Ó Ríordáin stole the notion of 'Faoistin' (confession) and 'Peaca' (sin), reworking these words until they became artistic terms. Joyce's surrender to 'the whatness of a thing' is recapitulated in Ó Ríordáin's desire to achieve 'instress' with his objects. Thus, for Ó Ríordáin in his poems, *I* becomes *Thou*, and every seeming opposite is revealed to be a secret double. Turnbull becomes his horse, and the horse Turnbull; a woman's eyes are reborn in her son's; male blends with female, the poet with his *anima*; and, of course, if Yeats's English poems are also a part of the Gaelic tradition in 'translation', then Ó Ríordáin's may, with equal validity, be seen as an experiment with the English tradition. There are times when creation *ex nihilo* seems to this particular poet but a polite phrase for the process of pillaging English:

A Ghaeilge im pheannsa
Do shinsear ar chaillis?
An teanga bhocht thabhartha
Gan sloinne tú, a theanga?

An leatsa na briathra
Nuair a dheinimse peaca?
Nuair is rúnmhar mo chroíse
An tusa a thostann?

O Gaelic in my pen
Have you lost your ancestry?
Are you a poor illegitimate,
Without surname, o language.

Are the verbs yours
When I commit a sin?
When my heart is secret,
Is it you who are quiet?

The poet who began by writing sprung rhythms in imitation of Hopkins finally concedes that his ideas are often stolen from the very language which he seeks only to escape:

Ag súrac atáirse
Ón striapach allúrach
Is sínim chugat smaointe
a ghoideas-sa uaithi.

You are escaping from
The foreign harlot
And I proffer to you the ideas
Which I stole from her.

The chauvinism underlying the word 'harlot' may offend some; but in general terms, these lines are a graphic illustration of the cultural trap described by Daniel Corkery as facing every Irish schoolchild in the 1920s and 1930s: 'No sooner does the child begin to use his intellect than what he learns begins to undermine, to weaken and to harass his emotional nature. For practically all that he reads is English . . . Instead of sharpening his own gaze on his neighbourhood, his reading distracts it'. Ó Ríordáin's poems bear palpable traces of his readings of Hopkins, Eliot and Wordsworth. In this context, Corkery's bitter attack on 'the want of native moulds' in Anglo-Irish writing seems extremely ironic, especially in view of his rather naïve recommendation of the Irish language as the natural remedy for such a lack. The diagnosis offered by Corkery had been astute when he said of the aspiring poet that 'his education provides him with an alien medium through which he is henceforth to look at his native land'. But Corkery's mistake was to believe that Irish was, by some mysterious privilege, immune to the incursions of international culture and modern thought. Ó Ríordáin suffered from no such delusion, but steeped himself in post-Christian philosophy, thereby disproving not only the chauvinist theories of Corkery, but also the defeatist assertion of Thomas

Kinsella that to write in Irish means 'the loss of contact with my own present . . . forfeiting a certain possible scope of language'.

Faced with the fact that most of his background reading was in English, Ó Ríordáin said that the best he could hope for was to deanglicise the material in his imagination, under the imprint of the Gaelic mind. This may be feasible for those to whom the Irish language comes more naturally than does English, but, in the case of other practitioners, Ó Direáin has said that what they produce by this means is all too often neither good Irish nor good poetry. This is the double bind experienced most notoriously by Yeats who wished to be counted one with Davis, Mangan and Ferguson; but who conceded at the end of his life that he owed his soul to Shakespeare, Spencer and William Morris, because all that he loved— including a wife—had come to him through English. And this is the plight of a writer like Michael Hartnett who bade farewell to English, only to find, in due course, that language is inescapable. In a poem to his English wife, he writes:

I abandoned English
but never you:
I have to hone my craft
in a wood that's new;
for my English grove
is naked, barren:
but I hope your day
of happiness is coming.
You'll have the silk of your heart one day,
We'll find us both our America.

That the option for Irish should culminate in a line which echoes John Donne is a perfect illustration of the constraints on the Gaelic poet.

So, although Anglo-Ireland and Gaelic Ireland may indeed have evolved quite separate cultures and traditions, they do, indeed, share what Conor Cruise O'Brien once called 'a common predicament.' It is thus quite proper to speak of Ó Ríordáin or Hartnett as Anglo-Irish authors, in the most literal sense of that term, for, just as much as Yeats or Synge, they also belong to a hyphenated literary tradition, with Gaelic and Anglo components. Apart from this common predicament, these writers share the sense of speaking for a dead tradition. The Gaelic poets, once dubbed 'voices from a hidden people', seem to speak, like the corpses in *Cré na Cille* or the voices in Beckett's trilogy, from the edge of the grave. Reading Ó Ríordáin, we have the sense of every lyric as a little death, when something of himself is expressed and lost, in a kind of grim rehearsal for death. In *Mise* he seems to suggest that his splintered selves will only be fully reintegrated 'on our deathbed'. In the meantime, the poem is as near as he can get, but it remains a marginal gloss on an unlivable, unknowable life. Ó Ríordáin's is a sensibility whose plight is to have lived through the consequences of its own extinction, even before it had a chance to know the self that died.

Many Gaelic poets seek in silence an escape from the stain of sounds, while conceding that sound is all they have. Like Beckett, they know that the search for the means to put an end to speech is what enables discourse to continue. Caitlín Maude repeatedly asks her interlocutor not to speak, while her own lines grow shorter and shorter. Ó Direáin's *Dínit an Bhróin* has the energy of its powerful reticence. Áine Ní Ghlinn, though verging on slack conversational prose, is actually a minimalist who equates caring with silence, loss with speech, and who follows Joyce in her predilection for the unfinished sentence. This is a technique especially appropriate to her world of echoes, filled by puzzling people who never quite constitute personalities, and personalities who never quite become characters. The trailing sentence is a fitting vehicle for people who can never quite become themselves.

This liminal state, of one who is neither dead nor living, neither poet nor proseperson, neither Irish nor English, neither male nor female, neither rational nor emotional, is the central zone of contemporary Gaelic poetry. Such destitution has its compensations, the most obvious being the opportunity it affords the poet to search for an absolute idiolect. The danger, of course, is of idiocy in the root-meaning of that word, of becoming a hopelessly private person who acknowledges no social debts.

Such boundary states, wherein both mind and body are annulled, are grist to the Buddhist's mill, for Buddhism, unlike the west, delights in contradictions. Gabriel Rosenstock has an eastern relish for silence. He floods words with space, divesting them of all context and freeing them from their traditional moorings, in hopes of rediscovering their pristine value. On the principle that 'every word was once a poem', he produces vertical lyrics deliberately designed to slow down the reading or recitation. He deploys the techniques of meditation in a Beckettesque manner with an unfinishable sentence. If Ní Ghlinn's personae are half-constructed persons, Rosenstock's, in the main, do not even aspire to the bogus glamour of being dispossessed of personality. A sense of self is something they can gladly do without, for they are mystically large enough to contain multitudes. Genius here becomes not an identity, but a capacity to take on the identity of every person or thing that lives. The poem is less an artefact than a radiant absence, which implies but never achieves its true correlative in the real world, an authentic lyric. Like the Whitman who sent those who would understand him to the nearest drop of water, Rosenstock can advise us, in *The Search*, to find his poems in rivers, clouds, stars.

The boundary between me and not-me in such poems disappears, as the distance between text and world is drastically reduced. If the person is a part of speech, then speech is also a part of the person. The dream of the 1960s—the eclipse of all distance and distinction—is complete.

The dangers of such poetry are manifest in the notorious illnesses and early deaths of many American exponents, as well as in the vagueness and diffuseness of much of their literary remains. Davitt and Rosenstock share with Ginsberg and Corso a love of the list, an inventory of the endless opulence of created things. There is something very American about this exhibition of affluence. It can all too easily seem another case of conspicuous western consumption rather than serene eastern impassiveness in the face of the world's variousness; but, of course, there is adequate sanction for it in the lyrical lists and inventories of synonyms which characterise the Gaelic poetic tradition. At times, such lists may lead only to the banality parodied by Flann O'Brien ('I am a flower in the wind. I am a hole in the wall') or lambasted in Whitman:

Over-Whitmanated song
That will not scan:
With adjectives laid end to end,
Extol the doughnut and commend
The common man.

The deeper danger of a poetry where subject becomes object, and all distinctions are obliterated, is the tendency to a deadly narcissism. This is less a problem for Davitt and Rosenstock than for some of their contemporaries. If Gaeilgeoirí have betrayed a fatal propensity to naval-gazing and to writing incessantly about the state of Gaeldom, then their poets seem, at times, incapable of writing about anything except the act of writing poetry. Where once the bards, or even the senior contemporary figures like Ó Direáin, Ó Tuairisc and Mhac an tSaoi could aim satiric barbs at a deserving enemy, now we are confronted by a gentler generation whose deepest wounds are self-inflicted. They find in art the source of their disease, as well as its diagnosis. Rosenstock's obsession with Billy Holiday is a tell-tale, as well as a brilliant, instance:

> You squeezed pain
> From the height of sweetness
> Sweetness
> From the height of pain.
> When you were raped
> At ten years old
> That was the first nail
> In the crucifixion of your race, your
>   womanhood
> And your art,
> Till in the end
> Your own voice frightened you
> Lady in satin.

It could be as near as Rosenstock will ever get to writing *An Ghaelig Mhilis Bhinn*, for, in the fate of the jazz-singer he seems to read his own. If your own voice is so frightening, then perhaps it is better to be a phoney-man, a skull filled with echoes.

Yet the poem *is* powerful, precisely because it senses that self-hatred, rather than self-love, is the actual basis of such narcissism. It is less an example than an indictment of the illness which it diagnoses. If the signs of that illness were apparent even in some of the most powerful Gaelic poems of the previous generation, then the cure may be found in the uncompromising self-criticism to which such self-scrutiny finally leads. James Joyce once complained that Gaelic enthusiasts did not care what banalities a writer uttered, just as long as he uttered them in their precious language; but today's Gaelic poets are strong and brave enough to insist on the most candid of criticism. They stake their claim as artists rather than as Gaelic-speakers. That they should be the first generation in the twentieth century to do this gives them, and us, infinite grounds for hope.

MÁIRTÍN Ó DIREÁIN

Máirtín Ó Direáin was born in 1910 on Inismore, the largest
of the Aran Islands. The publication, at his own expense, of
the pamphlets *Coinnle Geala* (1940) and *Dánta Aniar (1943)*,
by breaking with traditional verse forms, marks the begin-
ning of contemporary poetry in Irish. Awarded an Honorary
D Litt (National University of Ireland 1977), he has received
many prizes for his poetry. He died in 1988.

Faoiseamh A Gheobhadsa

Faoiseamh a gheobhadsa
Seal beag gairid
I measc mo dhaoine
Ar oileán mara,
Ag siúl cois cladaigh
Maidin is tráthnóna
Ó Luan go Satharn
  Thiar ag baile.

Faoiseamh a gheobhadsa
Seal beag gairid
I measc mo dhaoine,
Ó chrá croí,
Ó bhuairt aigne,
Ó uaigneas duairc,
Ó chaint ghontach,
  Thiar ag baile.

I will find solace

I will find solace
For a short time only
Among my people
On a sea-girt island,
Walking the shore
Morning and evening
Monday to Saturday
    In my western homeland.

I will find solace
For a short time only
Among my people,
From what vexes the heart,
From a troubled mind,
From soured solitude,
From wounding talk,
    In my western homeland.

Translated by Tomás Mac Síomóin

and Douglas Sealy

Maith Dhom

I m'aonar dom aréir,
I mo shuí cois mara,
An spéir ar ghannchuid néal
Is muir is tír faoi chalm,
Do chumraíocht ríonda
A scáiligh ar scáileáin m'aigne
Cé loinnir deiridh mo ghrá duit
Gur shíleas bheith in éag le fada.

Ghlaos d'ainm go ceanúil
Mar ba ghnách liomsa tamall,
Is tháinig scread scáfar
Ó éan uaigneach cladaigh;
Maith dhom murarbh áil leat
Fiú do scáil dhil i m'aice,
Ach bhí an spéir ar ghannchuid néal
Is muir is tír faoi chalm.

Forgive Me

Alone last night
And sitting on the strand,
The sky was sparse of cloud
And sea and land becalmed,
Your queenly form
Shadowed the screen of my mind,
This last flicker of my love for you
That I thought was dead a long time.

I fondly called your name
As I used to once,
And heard only the frightened screech
Of a lonely shorebird;
Forgive me if you did not wish
Even your dear shadow at my hand,
But the sky was sparse of cloud
And sea and land becalmed.

Translated by Gabriel Fitzmaurice

16th Irish
courtly Rom. tradition

Aisling

5

Dínit An Bhróin

Nochtaíodh domsa tráth
Dínit mhór an bhróin,
Ar fheiceáil dom beirt bhan
Ag siúl amach ó shlua
I bhfeisteas caointe dubh
Gan focal astu beirt:
D'imigh an dínit leo
Ón slua callánach mór.

Bhí freastalán istigh
Ó línéar ar an ród,
Fuadar faoi gach n-aon,
Gleo ann is caint árd;
Ach an bheirt a bhí ina dtost,
A shiúil amach leo féin
I bhfeisteas caointe dubh,
D'imigh an dínit leo.

The Dignity of Grief

Grief's great dignity
Was revealed to me once,
On seeing two women
Emerging from a crowd
In black mourning
Each without a word:
Dignity left with them
From the large and clamorous throng.

A tender was in
From a liner in the roads,
And everyone was rushing,
There was tumult and loud talk;
But the pair who were silent
Who walked out on their own
In black mourning
Left with dignity.

Translated by Gabriel Fitzmaurice

Ár Ré Dhearóil

Tá cime romham
Tá cime i mo dhiaidh,
Is mé féin ina lár
I mo chime mar chách,
Ó d'fhágamar slán
Ag talamh, ag trá,
Gur thit orainn
Crann an éigin.

Cár imigh an aoibh,
An gáire is an gnaoi,
An t-aiteas úrchruthach naíonda?
Gan súil le glóir,
Le héacht inár dtreo
Ná breith ar a nóin ag éinne.

Níl a ghiodán ag neach
Le rómhar ó cheart,
Níl éan ag ceol
Ar chraobh dó,
Ná sruthán ag crónán
Go caoin dó.

Tá cime romham
Tá cime i mo dhiaidh,
Is mé féin ina lár
I mo chime mar chách,
Is ó d'fhágamar slán
Ag talamh, ag trá,
Bíodh ár n-aird
Ar an Life chianda.

Our Wretched Era

A prisoner before me
A prisoner behind,
I stand between
A prisoner like all,
Since we said goodbye
To field, to strand,
Since we bent under
Necessity's yoke.

Where has cheerfulness gone,
The laughter and the liking,
The spontaneous child-like joy?
No hope of renown,
No scope for valour
And none has time for the evening prayer.

None has his plot
To dig of right,
No bird is singing
To him from a branch
Nor stream murmuring
Gently to him.

A prisoner before me,
A prisoner behind,
I stand between
A prisoner like all,
And since we said goodbye
To field, to strand,
Let us turn our minds
To the ancient Liffey.

Bíodh ár n-aire
Ar an abhainn
Ar an óruisce lán
A chuireann slán
Le grian deiridh nóna.

Bímis umhal ina láthair
Is i láthair an tsrutha
Is samhail den bheatha
Ach gur buaine,
Mar is samhail an abhainn
De shráid an tslua
Ach gur uaisle.

An lá is ionann ag mná
Faiche is sráid,
Páirc, trá, is grianán,
Ná bíodh cime gnáis
Gann faoi dhearbhdhíona:

Tá fairsinge díobh ann
Mar luaim thíos i mo dhiaidh iad,
Is deirid lucht cáis
Nach bhfuilid gan bhrí leo —

An macha cúil
Tráthnóna Sathairn,
An cluiche peile,
An imirt chártaí
Is ósta na bhfear
Ina múchtar cásamh.

Let us turn our attention
To the river
To the brimming golden water
That bids farewell
To the late evening sun.

Let us be humble in its presence
And in the presence of the moving water,
A symbol of life
But more enduring,
For the river is an image
Of the crowded street
But more sublime.

When women make no distinction
Between greensward and street
Meadow, strand and summer-house,
Let not the prisoner of convention
Be short of asylums:

There are plenty of them,
I list them below
And the compassionate say
They have their uses —

The back-garden
On Saturday evening,
The game of football,
The session at cards,
And the men's bar
Where complaint is quenched.

*asylums
for
prisoner
of convention*

11

Crot a athar thalmhaí
Do shúil ghrinn is léir,
Ag teacht ar gach fear
Atá i meán a laethe,
A chneadaíonn a shlí chun suíocháin
I mbus tar éis a dhinnéir.

Ní luaifear ar ball leo
Teach ná áras sinsir,
Is cré a muintire
Ní dháilfear síos leo,
Ach sna céadta comhad
Beidh lorg pinn leo.

Is a liacht fear acu
A chuaigh ag roinnt na gaoise
Ar fud páir is meamraim,
Ag lua an fhasaigh,
An ailt, an achta.

Is a liacht fear fós
A thug comhad leis abhaile,
Is cúram an chomhaid
In áit chéile chun leapa.

Is mná go leor
A thriall ina n-aice
Ar thóir an tsó,
An áilleagáin intrigh;
Galar a n-óghachta
A chuaigh in ainseal orthu
A thochrais go dóite
Abhras cantail.

The gait of his rural father
Can be seen by a sharp eye,
Overtaking each man
In middle-age
As he sighs his way to a seat
In the after-dinner bus.

Soon no one will trace them
To house or ancestral mansion,
And to the earth of their kin
They will not be committed,
But hundreds of files
Will bear the mark of their pen.

So many men among them
Dissipated their talents
On paper and parchment,
Citing the precedent,
Paragraph, decree.

And so many other men
Took a folder home with them
And the care of the folder
To their wifeless bed.

And many women
Journeyed beside them
In quest of luxury,
The merry-go-round;
The disease of their virginity
Turned chronic
And they bitterly wound
A fretful thread.

13

Mná eile fós
Ba indúilmheara ag feara,
Ba féile faoi chomaoin
Ba ghainne faoi chairéis,
A roinn a gcuid go fairsing
I ngéaga an fhir
Ba luaithe chucu
Ar chuairt amhaille,
Ar scáth an ghrá
Nár ghrá in aon chor
Ach aithris mhagaidh air,
Gan ualach dá éis
Ach ualach masmais.

Na hainmhithe is na héin
Nuair a fhaighid a gcuid dá chéile,
Ní gach ceann is luaithe chucu
A ghlacaid in aon chor.

I gcúiteamh an tsíl
Nach ndeachaigh ina gcré,
I gcúiteamh na gine
Nár fhás faoina mbroinn,
Nár iompair trí ráithe
Faoina gcom,
Séard is lú mar dhuais acu
Seal le teanga iasachta
Seal leis an ealaín,
Seal ag taisteal
Críocha aineola,
Ag cur cártaí abhaile
As Ostend is Paris,
Gan eachtra dála
Ar feadh a gcuarta,

Yet other women
Most alluring to men,
Most generous in bestowal,
Most niggard of scruple,
Lavished their all
In the arms of the man
Who first approached them
On a sly visit,
On the pretext of love
That wasn't love at all
But a mocking counterfeit,
With no consequent burden
But a burden of loathing.

Birds and beasts
When they couple together,
The firstcomer's not always the one
They decide to take.

To compensate for the seed
That did not enter their flesh,
To compensate for the child
That did not grow in their womb,
That they didn't carry nine months
In the hollow of their bodies,
The least they'd accept as dowry
Was a spell at foreign languages,
A spell at the arts,
A spell touring
In foreign parts,
Sending home postcards
From Ostend and Paris,
Without one loving encounter
In all their journeys,

Ná ríog ina dtreo
Ach ríog na fuaire.
Tá cime romham
Tá cime i mo dhiaidh,
Is mé féin ina lár
I mo chime mar chách,
Is a Dhia mhóir
Fóir ar na céadta againn,
Ó d'fhágamar slán
Ag talamh ag trá,
Tóg de láimh sinn
Idir fheara is mhná
Sa chathair fhallsa
Óir is sinn atá ciontach
I bhásta na beatha,
Is é cnámh ár seisce
Is é cnámh gealaí
Atá ar crochadh thuas
I dtrá ár bhfuaire
Mar bhagairt.

Knowing no grip
But the grip of apathy.
A prisoner before me
A prisoner behind,
I stand between them
A prisoner like all,
And Almighty God
Succour the hundreds of us
Since we said goodbye
To field, to strand,
Take us by the hand
Both men and women
In the deceitful city
For we are the guilty ones
Wasting life —
The bone of our sterility
Is the bone moon
That hangs above
In the strand of our apathy
As a portent.

quite Romantic

*Translated by Tomás Mac
Síomóin and Douglas Sealy*

~~family values~~

SEÁN Ó RÍORDÁIN

Seán Ó Ríordáin was born in Baile Bhúirne, Co. Cork, in 1917. One of the major Irish poets of the twentieth century, he published only three books of poetry and one book of translations (into modern Irish) of Irish religious poetry of the ninth to the twelfth century—in his lifetime. He died in 1977. A fifth volume, *Tar Éis Mo Bháis* (*After My Death*), was published posthumously in 1978.

Oileán Agus Oileán Eile

1: *Roimh Dhul ar Oileán Bharra Naofa*

Tá Sasanach ag iascaireacht sa loch,
Tá an fhírinne rólom ar an oileáin,
Ach raghad i measc na gcuimhne agus na gcloch,
Is nífead le mórurraim mo dhá láimh.

Raghad anonn is éistfead san oileán,
Éistfead seal le smaointe smeara naomh
A thiomnaigh Barra Naofa don oileáin,
Éistfead leo in inchinn an aeir.

11: *Amhras iar nDul ar an Oileán*

A Bharra, is aoibhinn liom aoibhneas do thí
Agus caraimse áitreabh do smaointe,
Ach ní feas dom an uaitse na smaointe
    airím
Mar tá daoscar ar iostas im intinn.

An Island and Another Island

1: Before Going on Saint Barra's Island

An Englishman is fishing in the lake,
On the island the naked truth is found,
But out among the memories and stones I'll stray
And wash my hands with reverence profound.

I will go and listen to the island sounds,
I will listen for the subtle thoughts of saints,
The legacy that Barra left upon this holy mound,
I will hear them in the instincts of the air.

ll: Doubt After Going on the Island

O Barra, sweet to me the sweetness of your home,
Where dwelt your thoughts it is my joy to be,
But wonder sometimes if the thoughts are yours or
    mine alone,
Born of the rot lodged deep in me.

Le bréithe gan bhrí,
Le bodhaire na mblian,
Thuirling clúmh liath
Ar mo smaointe.

Mar chloich a cúnlaíodh
Do hadhlacadh iad,
Do truailleadh a gclaíomh
Im intinn.

Naoimh is leanaí
A bhogann clúmh liath
De cheannaithe Chríost
Nó de smaointe.

Tá an t-aer mar mhéanfaíoch
Ar m'anam 'na luí,
Bhfuil Barra sa ghaoith
Am líonadh?

Tá Barra is na naoimh
Na cianta sa chria
Is dalladh púicín
Ad bhíogadh.

Tá tuirse im chroí
Den bhfocal gan draíocht,
Bíodh dalladh nó diabhal
Am shiabhradh.

With pointless talk,
And deafness down the years
My mind purblind
Became a thing diseased.

As stone interred in moss
My thoughts became,
Their sharpness dulled,
They were a blunted blade.

In saints and children
Christ's own face we see,
And in their thinking
Thought's true face appears.

The air is drowsy
On my listless spirit,
Is it Barra within the wind
That seeks to fill it?

Barra and his saints
Have long since passed from here,
It is confusion
That works in you, I fear;

I am heart-weary now
Of words banal,
Whether of blindness born
Or devil's plan.

lll: An Bíogadh

Tá ráflaí naomh san aer máguaird
Is an ghaoth ag fuáil tríd,
Tá paidir sheanda im chuimhne i
    léig,
Is mo smaointe á séideadh arís.

Anseo ar bhuaile smaointe naomh
Do léim chugham samhail nua,
Do chuala tarcaisne don saol
I nguth an éin bhí 'clagar ceoil.

An ceol a raid sé leis an mbith
Dob shin oileán an éin,
Níl éinne beo nach bhfuair oileán,
Is trua a chás má thréig.

lV: Oileán Gach Éinne

I bhfírinne na haigne
Tá oileán séin,
Is tusa tá ar marthain ann
Is triall fád dhéin,
Ná bíodh ort aon chritheagla
Id láthair féin,
Cé go loiscfidh sé id bheatha tú,
Do thusa féin,
Mar níl ionat ach eascaine
A dúirt an saol,
Níl ionat ach cabaireacht
Ó bhéal go béal:
Cé gur cumadh tú id phaidir gheal
Ar bhéal Mhic Dé

III: The Quickening

The tales of saints are round us in this place,
As the wind threads through them in the air,
In my memory there stirs an old and half-forgotten
    prayer,
And thoughts rekindled are breathing there.

An image new sprang to me in this place,
Here where were harvested the dreams of saints,
I heard a bird whose singing flayed the air
Abuse with bitter scorn the life we've made.

The bird's own song his island was, I swear,
The music that he flung into the world's face,
Each being was given an island there to reign,
And woe to him who does not there remain!

IV: Each One's Island

In the truth that is within the mind
There is a place serene,
An island hermitage where you must dwell
And seek your inmost being,
Tremble not when you with you
Come face to face,
Though the fire you are
Consume you in its rage,
For you are but a curse
The world flung about,
An aimless chattering
That goes from mouth to mouth:
Though first you came a shining prayer
By God's Son spoken,

Do scoiltis-se do thusa ceart
Le dúil sa tsaol,
Ach is paidir fós an tusa sin
Ar oiléan séin,
A fhan go ciúin ag cogarnach
Ar bheolaibh Dé
Nuair do rincis-se go macnasach
Ar ghob an tsaoil.

V: Oileán Bharra Naofa

Tráthnóna ceathach sa Ghuagán,
Ceo ag creimeadh faille,
Do chuardaíos comhartha ar oileán,
Do fuaireas é i gcrannaibh.

Im thimpeall d'eascair crainn chasfháis,
Dob achrannach a leagan,
Do lúbadar 'ngach uile aird
Mar chorp á dhó ina bheatha.

Mar scríbhinn breacaithe ar phár
Is scríbhinn eile trasna air
Chonac geanc is glún is cruit is spág,
Fá dheoidh chonac dealramh Gandhi.

A Bharra, chím i lúib na ngéag
Gur troideadh comhrac aonair
Idir thusa Dé is tusa an tsaoil
Anseo id gheanclainn naofa.

Nuair ghlanann ceo na fola léi
Tig áilleacht ait i rocaibh,
Is féidir cló a mheas ann féin
Sa tsolas cnámhach folamh.

With wordly love the you He made
You've rent and broken,
Still on your island
You remained a prayer,
Still quietly whispered
On God's lips there,
While you unheeding
Danced the world's way.

V: Saint Barra's Island

An evening full of rain in Gougane Barra,
The mist devoured each rock and each ravine,
I sought a sign somewhere within the island,
And found it in the trees.

Around me sprang the gnarled trees all twisted,
Distorted and convulsing they appeared,
As a living being within a furnace burning,
This way and that they writhed and heaved.

A script across a parchment I saw stumbling,
Across that script another script appeared,
I saw a nose, a knee, a hump, a foot ungainly,
And then saw Ghandi's image in a tree.

O Barra, in the branches was a message
That once was fought a duel where I stood
Between God's you and you the world's minion,
In the misshapen sanctuary of your wood.

When the mist that is the flesh disperses
A beauty strange in furrowed things we find,
One knows truth beyond the mirage of appearance
In the skeletal emptiness of the light.

Tá sult na saoirse i gcló na gcrann
Is grá don tsúil a fiaradh,
Tá dúil sa rud tá casta cam
Is gráin don bhog is don díreach.

Is fireann scríbhinn seo na gcrann,
Níl cíoch ná cuar in an bhall,
Tá manach scríte abhus is thall,
Sé Barra lúb na ngéag seo.

A insint féin ar Fhlaitheas Dé,
Ag sin oileán gach éinne,
An Críost atá ina fhuil ag scéith
An casadh tá ina bhréithre.

Is macasamhail dá oileán féin
Oileán seo Bharra Naofa,
An Críost a bhí ina fhuil ag scéith
An phúcaíocht ait i ngéagaibh.

VI: *An Sasanach agus Mé Féin*

Tá Sasanach ag iascaireacht sa loch
Is measaimse gur beag leis an t-oileán,
Ach ní feasach dom nach iascaireacht ar loch
Don Sasanach bheith ionraic ar oileán.

Raghad anonn is fágfad an t-oileán,
Fágfad slán le smaointe smeara naomh,
Raghad ag ceilt na fírinne mar chách,
Raghad anonn ag cabaireacht sa tsaol.

In the shapes of trees there is the joy of freedom.
There is love for him who follows their caprice,
In what is bent and convoluted there is pleasure,
There is rejection here for what's orderly and neat.

The tree-script is a masculine creation,
Neither breast nor curve in any place appears,
Monk is written in the forest all around us,
And Barra in the bendings of the trees.

A personal perception of God's heaven,
That is each one's island, one's retreat,
The Christ that in his blood is bleeding
Gives shape and purpose to his speech.

The island where lived the sainted Barra
Is an image of each man's island soul,
The Christ that in his blood was bleeding
Is the hauntings in the branches we behold.

VI: *The Englishman and Myself*

An Englishman is fishing in the lake near-by,
Of the island he seems almost unaware,
Perhaps he's found his island's own integrity
Fishing in the waters of the lake.

I will go and turn my back upon the island,
The subtle thoughts of saints I'll leave behind,
I will go concealing truth as do the others,
I will go gossiping in the taverns of life.

Translated by Muiris Ó Ríordáin

Cnoc Mellerí

Sranntarnach na stoirme i Mellerí aréir
Is laethanta an pheaca bhoig mar bhreoiteacht
    ar mo chuimhne,
Laethanta ba leapacha de shonaschlúmh an tsaoil
Is dreancaidí na drúise iontu ag preabarnaigh ina
    mílte.

D'éirigh san oíche sídhe gaoithe coiscéim,
Manaigh ag triall ar an Aifreann,
Meidhir, casadh timpeall is rince san aer,
Bróga na manach ag cantaireacht.

Bráthair sa phroinnteach ag riaradh suipéir,
Tost bog ba bhalsam don intinn,
Ainnise naofa in oscailt a bhéil,
Iompar mothaolach Críostaí mhaith.

Do doirteadh steall anchruthach gréine go mall
Trí mhúnla cruiceogach fuinneoige,
Do ghaibh sí cruth manaigh ó bhaitheas go bonn
Is do thosnaigh an ghrian ag léitheoireacht.

Leabhar ag an manach bán namhdach á léamh,
Go hobann casachtach an chloig,
Do múchadh an manach bhí déanta de ghréin
Is do scoilteadh an focal 'na phluic.

Mount Mellery

The storm was growling loud last night round
      Mellery,
Within was sin languid and leprous sprawled
      across my memory,
In down-soft beds of self-indulgence I had lain
Where lusts like bed-lice stung my loins awake.

Into the night-time flowed enchantment sweet,
The numerous murmur of the Mass-going feet,
Monks joyous came, and joy danced on the air,
And oh! rough sandals all were chanting prayers.

A brother had at supper waited on the guests,
The quiet soothed the minds that could not rest,
A saintly awkwardness within his speech appeared,
His Christian bearing full of simple dignity.

Misshapen sunlight thro' the window came,
Assuming the window's antique curve and shape,
It then became a monk from top to toe—
The sunlight read its office by the door.

The monk, all sinister and white, read from his page
Until a sudden clock croaked in that cloistered place,
The sun-made monk was then no longer there,
Dumbfounded! Quenched! Erased!

Buaileadh clog Complin is bhrostaigh gach aoi
Maolchluasach i dtreo an tséipéil;
Bhí beatha na naomh seo chomh bán le braitlín
Is sinne chomh dubh leis an daol.

Allas ar phaidrín brúite im láimh,
Mo bhríste dlúth-tháite lem ghlúin,
Ghluais sochraid chochallach manach thar bráid,
Ba shuarach leat féachaint a thabhairt.

Ach d'fhéachas go fiosrach gan taise gan trua
Mar fhéachadar Giúdaigh fadó
Ar Lazarus cúthail ag triall as an uaigh
Is géire na súl thart á dhó.

Do thiteadar tharainn 'na nduine is 'na nduine,
Reilig ag síorphaidreoireacht,
Is do thuirling tiubhscamall de chlúimh liath na cille
Go brónach ar ghrua an tráthnóna.

'Tá an bás ag cur seaca ar bheatha anseo,
Aige tá na manaigh ar aimsir,
Eisean an tAb ar a ndeineann siad rud,
Ar a shon deinid troscadh is tréadhanas.

'Buachaill mar sheanduine meirtneach ag siúl,
Masla ar choimirce Dé,
An té 'dhéanfadh éagóir dá leithéid ar gharsún
Do chuirfeadh sé cochall ar ghréin;

The bell for compline called, and every guest
Hurried to take his place among the rest,
Each was aware he moved where saints abided
While he himself was black as hell inside him.

Perspiration from my hands was on my beads,
My trouser-legs pulled tight about my knees,
A funeral of hooded monks went by,
It seemed a sacrilege to raise one's eyes.

But look I did with shameless curiosity, I know,
As did the Jews at Lazarus long ago,
When from the tomb self-consciously he came
Into the burning light of eyes amazed.

They passed us, one by one they passed us by,
A churchyard full of prayers eternally,
A thick cloud came like mildew from the grave
And settled darkly on the evening's face.

'Death like frostbite killing life is here,
The monks no more than servants to his will appear,
He is their Abbot, him they all obey,
At his whim they fast and they abstain.

'See that young man, an old man's is his gait,
An insult to the God who loves and cares,
The person who would on a youth inflict such wrong
Would put the sun in purdah before long;

'Do scaipfeadh an oíche ar fud an mheán lae,
Do bhainfeadh an teanga den abhainn,
Do chuirfeadh coir drúise in intinn na n-éan
Is do líonfadh le náire an domhan.

'Tá an buachaill seo dall ar an aigne fhiáin
A thoirchíonn smaointe éagsúla,
Gan bacadh le hAb ná le clog ná le riail
Ach luí síos le smaoineamh a dhúile.

'Ní bhlaisfidh sé choíche tréanmheisce mná
A chorraíonn mar chreideamh na sléibhte,
'Thug léargas do Dante ar Fhlaitheas Dé
      tráth,
Nuair a thuirling na haingil i riocht véarsaí,'

Sin é dúirt an ego bhí uaibhreach easumhal,
Is é dallta le feirg an tsaoil,
Ach do smaoiníos ar ball, is an ceol os ár gcionn,
Gur mó ná an duine an tréad.

D'fhéachas laistiar díom ar fhásach mo shaoil,
Is an paidrín brúite im dhóid,
Peaca, díomhaointeas is caiteachas claon,
Blianta urghránna neantóg.

D'fhéachas ar bheatha na manach anonn,
D'aithníos dán ar an dtoirt,
Meadaracht, glaine, doimhinbhrí is comhfhuaim,
Bhí m'aigne cromtha le ceist.

Would seek to scatter night across the day,
Would rob the singing river of its lay,
Would charge the birds with ugliness and lust,
Would fill the world with shame and with disgust.

That boy knows nothing of the untamed mind,
The mind that breeds a thousand thoughts run wild,
The mind that cares not jot for Abbot, rule or time,
But loves to lie within the arms of his desire.

Never will he be drunk with woman's love,
That love that can as faith the mountains move,
That love in which the heavens by Dante were
	perceived
When in the guise of verses the angels were revealed.'

Thus spoke the ego that was disdainful, proud,
A blind, resentful ego in the crowd,
But then I realised, as music filled the air,
That greater than the person is the race.

I turned to see the desert of my ways,
Within my sweaty hand the beads still lay,
Sin, idleness, I found, and perverse waste,
The ugly fruit of all my bitter days.

The monks across from me became a living poem,
I saw at once the beauty of their souls,
Order and innocence, and harmony profound,
The questions in my mind kept going round and round.

Do bhlaiseas mórfhuascailt na faoistine ar maidin,
Aiseag is ualach ar ceal,
Scaoileadh an t-ancaire, rinceas sa Laidin,
Ba dhóbair dom tuirling ar Neamh.

Ach do bhlaiseas, uair eile, iontaoibh asam féin,
Mo chuid fola ar fiuchadh le neart,
Do shamhlaíos gur lonnaigh im intinn Spiorad Naom
Is gur thiteadar m'fhocail ó Neamh.

Buarach ar m'aigne Eaglais Dé,
Ar shagart do ghlaofainn coillteán,
Béalchráifeacht an Creideamh, ól gloine gan léan,
Mairfeam go dtiocfaidh an bás!

Manaigh mar bheachaibh ag fuaimint im
      cheann,
M'aigne cromtha le ceist,
Nótaí ag rothaíocht anonn is anall,
Deireadh le Complin de gheit.

Sranntarnach na stoirme i Mellerí aréir
Is laethanta an pheaca bhoig mar bhreoiteacht
      ar mo chuimhne,
Is na laethanta a leanfaidh iad fá cheilt i ndorn Dé,
Ach greim fhir bháite ar Mhellerí an súgán seo
      filíochta.

Next morning I confessed my many sins,
Disgorged the horror that had been within,
No longer anchored to the earth was I,
Danced in the Latin up to heaven's height.

But then there came presumption to my door,
Within my blood there was a pulse of power,
It seemed a Holy Spirit came to rest within my heart,
And when I spoke I felt a man apart.

'The Church is spancelling my mind,' I cried,
'Priests are mere eunuchs,' that's what I divined,
'The Faith is lip-service, drink a glass,' I said,
'Eat, drink, be merry, for soon we will be dead.'

The monks like bees kept up the murmurous sound,
The questions in my mind kept going round and
        round,
The chanted notes from side to side were swaying,
Then suddenly the end of compline came.

The storm was growling loud last night round
        Mellery,
Within was sin languid and leprous sprawled across
        my memory,
The future lies in God's clenched hand I know,
But desperately I cling to Mellery by this, my wisp
        of poem.

Translated by Muiris Ó Ríordáin

Ceol Ceantair

Chuala sé an ceol i gcainteanna Dhún Chaoin,
Ní hiad na focail ach an fonn
A ghabhann trí bhlas is fuaimeanna na Mumhan,
An ceol a chloiseann an strainséir;
Ceol ceantair
Ná cloiseann lucht a labhartha,
Ceol nár chualasa riamh,
Toisc a ghiorracht dom is bhí,
Is mé bheith ar adhastar ag an mbrí.

Ceol a cloistear fós sa Mhumhain,
Fiú in áiteanna 'nar tréigeadh an chanúint.

Local Music

He heard the lilt in the language of Dún Chaoin,
Not the lyrics but the air
That goes through the sounds and flow of Munster,
The music the stranger hears;
A local music
That its speakers do not hear,
A music I never heard
Because I was so near
And I in harness to the sense.

A music you will hear in Munster yet
Even where they've abandoned dialect.
Translated by Gabriel Fitzmaurice

Malairt

'Gaibh i leith,' arsa Turnbull, 'go bhfeice tú an
    brón
    I súilibh an chapaill,
Dá mbeadh crúba chomh mór leo sin fútsa bheadh
    brón
      Id shúilibh chomh maith léis.'

Agus b'fhollas gur thuig sé chomh maith sin an brón
    I súilibh an chapaill,
Is gur mhachnaigh chomh cruaidh sin gur tomadh
     é fá dheoidh
    In aigne an chapaill.

D'fhéachas ar an gcapall go bhfeicinn an brón
    'Na shúilibh ag seasamh,
Do chonac súile Turnbull ag féachaint im threo
    As cloigeann an chapaill.

D'fhéachas ar Turnbull is d'fhéachas air fá dhó
    Is do chonac ar a leacain
Na súile rómhóra a bhí balbh le brón—
    Súile an chapaill.

A Change

'Come over,' said Turnbull, 'and look at the
      sorrow
   In the horse's eyes.
If you had hooves under you like
      those
   There would be sorrow in your eyes.'

And 'twas plain that he knew this sorrow so well
   In the horse's eyes
And he wondered so deeply that he dived in the
      end
   Into the horse's mind.

I looked at the horse then that I might see
   The sorrow in his eyes
And Turnbull's eyes were looking at me
   From the horse's mind.

I looked at Turnbull and looked once again
      And there in Turnbull's head —
Not Turnbull's eyes, but, dumb with grief,
   Were the horse's eyes instead.

Translated by Gabriel Fitzmaurice

Saoirse

Raghaidh mé síos i measc na ndaoine
De shiúl mo chos,
Is raghaidh mé síos anocht.

Raghaidh mé síos ag lorg daoirse
Ón mbinibshaoirse
Tá ag liú anseo:

Is ceanglód an chonairt smaointe
Tá ag drannadh im thimpeall
San uaigneas:

Is loirgeod an teampall rialta
Bhíonn lán de dhaoine
Ag am fé leith:

Is loirgeod comhluadar daoine
Nár chleacht riamh saoirse,
Ná uaigneas:

Is éistfead leis na scillingsmaointe,
A malartaítear
Mar airgead:

Is bhéarfad gean mo chroí do dhaoine
Nár samhlaíodh riamh leo
Ach macsmaointe.

Ó fanfad libh de ló is d'oíche,
Is beidh mé íseal,
Is beidh mé dílis
D'bhur snabsmaointe.

Freedom

I'll go down among the people
I'll go on foot
And I'll go down tonight.

I will go down bondage-seeking
From the venom-liberty
That's howling here:

And I will tie the thought-pack, wheeling
and snarling all around me
In my solitude:

And I will seek the ordered temple
That is full of people
At special times;

And I will seek the company of people
who never practised freedom
or solitude:

And shilling-thoughts I will be hearing
That are exchanged
Like money:

The love of my heart I'll give to people
Who never imagined
Other than the secondhand.

Oh, I will stay morning and evening,
And I'll be humble,
Faithful, obedient
To your stub-thoughts.

Mar do chuala iad ag fás im intinn,
Ag fás gan chuimse,
Gan mheasarthacht.

Is do thugas gean mo chroí go fíochmhar
Don rud tá srianta,
Do gach macrud:

Don smacht, don reacht, don teampall daoineach,
Don bhfocal bocht coitianta,
Don am fé leith:

Don ab, don chlog, don seirbhíseach,
Don chomparáid fhaitíosach,
Don bheaguchtach:

Don luch, don tomhas, don dreancaid bhídeach,
Don chaibidil, don líne,
Don aibítir:

Don mhórgacht imeachta is tíochta,
Don chearrbhachas istoíche,
Don bheannachtain:

Don bhfeirmeoir ag tomhas na gaoithe
Sa bhfómhar is é ag cuimhneamh
Ar pháirc eornan:

Don chomhthuiscint, don chomh-shean-
    chuimhne,
Do chomhiompar chomhdhaoine,
Don chomh-mhacrud.

In my mind these thoughts I hear them
Growing freely
Without moderation.

And I'll give my heart's love fiercely
To the thing that is bridled,
To every copied thing:

To discipline, law, the church full of people,
To the poor. common word,
To the special time:

To the abbot, the bell, the servant of people,
To the analogy that's fearful,
To courage that's meagre:

To the mouse, to measurement, to the tiny flea,
To the chapter, to the line,
To the alphabet:

To coming's and going's majesty,
To nightly cardgames,
To salutations:

To the farmer judging wind
In the autumn while he thinks
Of his barleyfield:

To the common understanding and tradition of
        a people,
To the common behaviour of equals,
To the endless imitation of their lives:

Is bheirim fuath anois is choíche
Do imeachtaí na saoirse
Don neamhspleáchas.

Is atuirseach an intinn
A thit in iomar doimhin na saoirse,
Ní mhaireann cnoc dar chruthaigh Dia ann,
Ach cnoic theibí, sainchnoic shamhlaíochta,
Is bíonn gach cnoc díobh lán de mhianta
Ag dreapadóireacht gan chomhlíonadh,
Níl teora leis an saoirse
Ná le cnoca na samhlaíochta,
Ná níl teora leis na mianta,
Ná faoiseamh
Le fáil.

For now and ever my hate has deepened
For the goings-on of freedom,
For independence.

That mind is weary
That fell in the trough of freedom,
God's hills do not exist there
But abstract hills of mind,
And every hill is full of desires
Which climb unfulfilled,
There's no limit to this freedom
Or to the hills of the mind
There's no limit to the desires
Nor any
Release.

Translated by Gabriel Fitzmaurice

Adhlacadh Mo Mháthar

Grian an Mheithimh in úllghort,
     Is siosarnach i síoda an tráthnona,
Beach mhallaithe ag portaireacht
     Mar screadstracadh ar an nóinbhrat.

Seanalitir shalaithe á léamh agam,
     Le gach focaldeoch dar ólas
Pian bhinibeach ag dealgadh mo chléibhse,
     Do bhrúigh amach gach focal díobh a dheoir
          féin.

Do chuimhníos ar an láimh a dhein an scríbhinn,
     Lámh a bhí inaitheanta mar aghaidh
Lámh a thál riamh cneastacht seana-
          Bhíobla,
     Lámh a bhí mar bhalsam is tú tinn.

Agus thit an Meitheamh siar isteach sa
          Gheimhreadh,
     Den úllghort deineadh reilig bhán cois
          abhann,
Is i lár na balbh-bháine i mo thimpeall
     Do liúigh os ard sa tsneachta an dúpholl.

Gile gearrachaile lá a céad chomaoine,
     Gile abhlainne Dé Domhnaigh ar
          altóir,
Gile bainne ag sreangtheitheadh as na
          cíochaibh,
     Nuair a chuireadar mo mháthair, gile
          an fhóid.

My Mother's Burial

June sun in the orchard
    And a silken rustling in the fading day,
An infernal bee humming
    Like a screamtearing of the evening's veil.

I was reading an old letter,
    And every word-drink I imbibed
Thorned my heart with bitter pain,
    At every single word I read,
      I cried.

I remembered then the hand that wrote the letter,
    A hand distinguishable as a face,
A hand which flowed with the meekness of an old
      Bible,
    A hand which was like balsam to my pain.

And then the June moved over into winter
    And the orchard became a white cemetery by a
      stream
And amid the dumb whiteness all around me
    Through the snow I could hear the black hole
      scream.

The brightness of a girl at her first Communion,
    The brightness of the host on Sunday on the
      altar of God,
The brightness of milk like string coming from an
      udder,
    When they buried my mother, the brightness
      of the sod.

Bhí m'aigne á sciúirseadh féin ag iarraidh
	An t-adhlacadh a bhlaiseadh go hiomlán.
Nuair a d'eitil tríd an gciúnas bán go míonla
	Spideog a bhí gan mhearbhall gan scáth:

Agus d'fhan os cionn na huaighe fé mar go
		mb'eol di
	Go raibh an toisc a thug í ceilte ar chách
Ach an té a bhí ag feitheamh ins an gcomhrainn,
	Is do rinneas éad fén gcaidreamh
		neamhghnách.

Do thuirling aer na bhFlaitheas ar an uaigh sin,
	Bhí meidhir uafásach naofa ar an
		éan,
Bhíos deighilte amach ón diamhairghnó im
		thuata,
	Is an uaigh sin os mo chomhair in imigéin.

Le cumhracht bróin do folcadh m'anam drúiseach,
	Thit snéachta geanmnaíochta ar mo chroí,
Anois adhlacfad sa chroí a deineadh ionraic
	Cuimhne na mná a d'iompair mé trí ráithe
		ina broinn.

Tháinig na scológa le borbthorann sluasad,
	Is do scuabadar le fuinneamh an chré isteach
		san uaigh,
D'fhéachas-sa treo eile, bhí comharsa ag glanadh a
		ghlúine,
	D'fhéachas ar an sagart is bhí saoltacht ina
		ghnúis.

While my mind was scourging itself with trying
	To taste my mother's burial, whole, complete,
Through the white silence flew so gently
	A robin, without confusion, without fear.

She remained above the grave as if knowing
	That the reason for her coming was concealed
		to all
But the one who was waiting in the coffin
	And I was jealous of this intimate, strange
		talk.

The air of Heaven descended on that grave there,
	There was an awful, holy mirth about that
		robin,
I was cut off from the mystery like a novice,
	The grave was far away though I was beside
		the coffin.

My lustful soul was cleansed with fragrant sorrow,
	The purity of snow fell on my heart,
In the heart that was made upright I will bury
	The memory of the woman who carried me for
		three seasons.

The strong men began with their rude shovels,
	And boldly swept the earth into her
		grave,
I looked the other way, a neighbour was brushing
	his knees clean,
		I looked at the priest and saw worldliness in his
		face.

Grian an Mheithimh in úllghort,
   Is siosarnach i síoda an tráthnóna,
Beach mhallaithe ag portaireacht
   Mar screadstracadh ar an nóinbhrat.

Ranna beaga bacacha á scríobh agam,
   Ba mhaith liom breith ar eireaball spideoige,
Ba mhaith liom sprid lucht glanta glún a dhíbirt,
   Ba mhaith liom triall go deireadh lae go
      brónach.

June sun in the orchard
    And a silken rustling in the fading day,
An infernal bee humming
    Like a screamtearing of the evening's veil.

I am writing small, uneven verses,
    I would like to catch a robin's tail,
I would like to dispel the knee-brushing spirit,
    To journey sadly to the end of day.

Translated by Gabriel Fitzmaurice

Súile Donna

Is léi na súile donna so
A Chím i bplaosc a mic,
Ba theangmháil le háilleacht é
A súile a thuirlingt ort;

Ba theangmháil phribhléideach é
Lena meabhair is lena corp,
Is míle bliain ba ghearr leat é,
Is iad ag féachaint ort.

Na súile sin gurbh ise iad,
Is ait liom iad aige,
Is náir liom aghaidh a thabhairt uirthi,
Ó tharla sí i bhfear.

Nuair b'ionann iad is ise dhom,
Is beag a shíleas-sa
Go bhfireannóidh na súile sin
A labhradh baineann liom

Cá bhfaighfí údar mearbhaill
Ba mheasa ná é seo?
An gcaithfeam malairt agallaimh
A chleachtadh leo anois?

Brown Eyes

These brown eyes I see are hers
Now in her son's head,
It was a thing most beautiful
That you inherited;

It was a meeting privileged
With her mind and body too,
For a thousand years would pass so swift
If they but looked at you.

Because these eyes belong to her
It's strange that he has them,
I'm ashamed to face her now because
They happened in a man.

When she and they were one to me
Little did I think
Those eyes would change to masculine
That spoke so womanly.

Where is the source of madness
That's any worse than this?
Do I have to change my dialogue
Now that they are his?

Ní hí is túisce a bhreathnaigh leo,
Ach an oiread lena mac,
Ná ní hé an duine deireanach
A chaithfidh iad dar liom.

Ab shin a bhfuil de shíoraíocht ann,
Go maireann smut dár mblas,
Trí bhaineannú is fireannú,
Ón máthair go dtí an mac?

She wasn't the first to see with them
Any more than he
Nor will he be the last
Who will wear them.

Is this all there is of eternity
That something of us lives on
Becoming masculine and feminine
From the mother to the son?

Translated by Gabriel Fitzmaurice

Cúl An Tí

Tá Tír na nÓg ar chúl an tí,
    Tír álainn trína chéile,
Lucht ceithre chos ag siúl na slí
    Gan bróga orthu ná léine,
    Gan Béarla acu ná Gaeilge.

Ach fásann clóca ar gach droim
    Sa tír seo trína chéile,
Is labhartar teanga ar chúl an tí
    Nár thuig aon fhear ach Aesop,
    Is tá sé siúd sa chré anois.

Tá cearca ann is ál sicín,
    Is lacha righin mhothaolach,
Is gadhar mór dubh mar namhaid sa tír
    Ag drannadh le gach éinne,
    Is cat ag crú na gréine.

Sa chúinne thiar tá banc dramhaíl'
    Is iontaisí an tsaoil ann,
Coinnleoir, búclaí, seanhata tuí,
    Is trúmpa balbh néata,
    Is citeal bán mar ghé ann.

Is ann a thagann tincéirí
    Go naofa, trína chéile,
Tá gaol acu le cúl an tí,
    Is bíd ag iarraidh déirce
    Ar chúl gach tí in Eirinn.

The Back of the House

At the back of the house is Fairyland—
    A lovely, anyhow place—
With four-footed creatures on every hand
    Completely shoeless and shirtless,
    Knowing no English nor Irish.

But on each one there grows a cloak—
    In that anyhow place of places—
And back of the house a language is spoken
    That no man could follow but Aesop,
    And he's in his grave a long day now.

There are some hens there and a clutch of chickens,
    And a duck like a simpleton,
And a big black dawg who raises the dickens
    Barking at everyone,
    And a cat milking the sun.

In that corner is the Bank of Things Put Away and
    That's-That,
    With its wonders unbelievable—
Wax candles, gold buckles, an old straw hat,
    A trumpet, dumb without battle,
    And, of all things, a white kettle.

There come the tinkers, kicking up no rows,
    But saintly, like Simple-Simons,
They are one kin with the back of the house
    And they come a-begging, their quiet hands
    At the back of each house in Ireland.

Ba mhaith liom bheith ar chúl an tí
Sa doircheacht go déanach
Go bhfeicinn ann ar chuairt gealaí
An t-ollaimhín sin Aesop
Is é ina phúca léannta.

At the back of the house I'd like to be
    In the darkness, in the lateness,
And perhaps on his moonlit visit I'd see
    Little Professor Aesop,
    That knowledgeable fairy.

Translated by David Marcus

EOGHAN Ó TUAIRISC

Eoghan Ó Tuairisc, (Eugene Watters) was born in Ballinasloe,
Co. Galway in 1919. Celebrated as an author in both Irish and
English, he wrote poetry, plays and novels. He received
many awards for his work. He was the first of the *Aosdána*
members to die. He died in Wexford in 1982.

Bóithre Bána
as *Lux Aeterna*

Is fada uaim na bóithre,
Na bóithre fada, bán faoin ngréin,
Siar thar choim na má móire
Go leisciúil leadránach ar strae.

In uaigneas caoin mo chuimhne
Cloisim naosc go géar gearr garbh
Amuigh i gciúnas na riasca
Ag buaireamh bhrionglóidí na marbh.

Asal dubh go smaointeach
Ag comhaireamh gach coiscéim dá shlí,
Cailín ard le cosa ríona
Ag tarraingt uisce i mbuicéidín.

Sráidbhaile ina chodladh
An deatach ina línte réidh,
Foscadh úr thar fráma dorais
Is cumhracht dí i mbrothall lae.

White Roads

from *Lux Aeterna*

These are the roads I miss
The long roads white in the sun
Meandering as they please
The middle of the great plain.

Forlorn, I gently call to mind
Out of the marsh's quiet mood
The snipe's voice sharp and wild
Troubling the dreaming dead.

A black donkey thoughtfully tallies
Every step his feet trail,
A tall girl with a queen's swagger
Draws water in a little pail.

A roadside village sleeps its thread
Of steady smoke into the air,
Doorways deep in welcome shade,
Regaling draughts in the heat of the day.

Siar arís an bóthar,
Ór á leá i mbarra géag,
Meisce mhilis an tráthnóna
Is an saol faoi dhraíocht ag dán an éin.

Uch, is fada uaim na bóithre,
Na bóithre atá bán faoin ngréin,
Is ó ghleo na cathrach móire
Éalaíonn mo chuimhne leo ar strae.

Further still on roads like these
Evening is sweetly long,
Gold turns liquid in the trees,
Life is snared in a bird's song.

Yes, I miss these paths and ways
These roads whitening in the sun:
It is down their miles my mind strays
Far beyond the city's din.

Translated by Conleth Ellis

Requiem as *Aifreann na Marbh*

Cuireann an clog teibí
Ticín cliste sa chiúnas
Ag fuascailt mhíshuaimhneas a sprionga sa
    dorchacht,
Ach filleann an fhilíocht ar an bhfile.

Creimeann luchóigín a cuid cáipéisí,
Tá tuiscint eile ar fad aicise
De mhíshuaimhneas na fiacaile ag cnaí sa dorchacht,
Ach luíonn an file ar a leaba feasa

Séidte.

Beidh sprionga na rithime fuascailte
Agus beidh an fhiacailín sásta
Den turas tochailte dá nead sa dorchacht,
Ach tá tuiscint eile den suaimhneas ag an bhfile

I bhfaoiseamh a rithime, tar éis a shaothair,
Agus déanann sé gáire dó féin mar cloiseann sé
Ina luí, súil bheo, sa dorchacht,
I dticín an chloig agus i sioscadh na fiacaile

Oídhe Chlainne Hiroshima.

Tagann suaimhneas anama
San Fhocal ag broinneadh ó chroí na dorchachta
Agus filleann an fhilíocht ar an bhfoinse

Requiem from *Mass of the Dead*

The clock abstractly stitches
An ingenious tick into the silence
Relieving in the dark its spring's unrest,
But the poem recoils on the poet.

A little mouse gnaws at her documents—
Different entirely is the view she takes
Of the tooth's unrest grinding in the dark—
But the poet lies on his bed of wisdom

At his last gasp.

The rhythm's tension will find release
And the small tooth will be happy
With its excavating a nest in the dark,
But the poet sees rest otherwise

In the relief of his rhythm, after his efforts,
And he smiles to himself as he hears
Lying alert in the dark
In the clock's ticking and the tooth's cutting

The tragedy of the children of Hiroshima.

Peace of mind comes
With the Word welling out of the heart of darkness
And the poem comes full circle to its course

Translated by Conleth Ellis

As *Dialann sa Díseart*

Grianlá
i gcuimhne ghloineata na habhann
cois droichid

na maidí fillte
ina dtost ar an seas
fanann na litreacha

hiaraiglificí
stampaí beaga gealdaite ag rá
tá áiteachaí

dual don droichead é féin
a scríobh ina thrasnú
gach cloch a compánach
thíos, gach loscán-líon
gach cuar á iomlánú

maide rámha ag bícearnach
rinn ghoib
tá an scríbhinn ríonda as a riocht

From *Diary in the Desert*

Sun-day
in the glazed mind of the river
by the bridge

the oars crossed
silent on the thwart
the letters waiting

hieroglyphics
small bright stamps saying
there are places.

It is in the bridge's nature
to sign itself in its crossing,
every stone with its partner
down below, every tadpole-bulge,
every curve made whole.

An oar squeaking
The point of a prow.
The script distorted beyond reading .

Translated by Conleth Ellis

Bestfield Lock

as *Dialann sa Díseart*

Bestfield Lock
gan taibhse, gan tairseach

nascaimid don tír, osclaimid
an dobhargheata gíoscanach
ualach an uisce ina dhord sleamhain
á líonadh, ár mbodhrú
as raon na gcluas orainn fanann an cheist

spéir
gan simléar
na stumpaí lofa, an déideadh ghlas
ár bpianadh i bpoll an iarta
tá an créachtach corcair ar ais
deireadh Lúnasa

iarann ar iarann ag clingeadh
comhlaí, rópaí
clingeann ár nguthanna san easpa mhór

ar bord, dínascadh, síos
síos sa duibheagán, an trínse cúng
ar snámh i bpuiteach na gcéadta a maistriú
gan taibhse gan tairiscint
glae agus glóthach ar an tseanéibhearchloch
stinks, Styx, sticks
san fhualuisce seo ag sláthairt
faigheann an teanga féin a bás

ar an sruth amach
aer úr
airgead bréagach don tsúil

Bestfield Lock

from *Diary in the Desert*

Bestfield Lock
not a flicker of life in the ruins

we tie up, we open
the creaking sluice
the water's burden a sleek drone
filling up, moidering us, putting
out of earshot the question that hangs on the air

not a chimney
on the skyline,
rotten stumps, a raw toothache
throbbing in the hole behind the hearth,
the purple loosestrife is back
this August end

iron ringing on iron,
gates, ropes
our voices hollow in the void

we board, we cast off, down
down into the abyss, the narrow trench
we float churning the mud of centuries
not a sinner in sight
slime, ooze on the ancient granite
stinks, Styx, sticks
slithering about in this sewer
even speech is left for dead

drifting out
lifegiving air
counterfeit coins for the eye

Translated by Conleth Ellis

As *Dialann sa Díseart*

Scoireann an clóscríobhán dá shealgaireacht
ag an lánstad deiridh. Ponc.
Leabhar eile ar an saol don saol
ach don údar foilmhe.

Dearcaim an tsíleáil den chadás geal
a dhearamar ina dhíon don cheardaíocht
saol eile, súilíocht eile,
dallta
mar lasadh coinnle i bhfianaise an lae

anuas, fadtuirseach, amach
i dtráthnóna as cuimse mór
i measc na saileog cois srutha agus buicéad liom
ar théad á líonadh
Tharraing, chonaic
an duilleog
sa bhuicéad ar snámh

aiteas éigin san fhoilmhe
beannacht san aer
gearr anois go mbeidh an bhliain ag dúnadh
chín lae a dialainne

cén meanga sin ar an taibhse béil sa bhuicéad

duilleog rua
chomh seang le teanga an chú.

From *Diary in the Desert*

The typewriter quits its foraging
on the last fullstop. Crux.
One more book born to the world
but only emptiness for the writer.

I eye the white cotton drape
we made into a shelter for crafting—
a different existence, other expectations
dimmed
like a candle lit in the full light of day.

Down, bone-weary, out
into an enormous evening
among the streamside willows
filling a bucket tied from a string,
I drew it up and saw
the leaf
afloat.

The emptiness somehow filled,
the air bearing a blessing,
not long now till the year will be fastening
the clasp of its diary.

Is that the flicker of a smile
on the mouthshape in the bucket?

A red leaf
lean as a hound's tongue.

Translated by Conleth Ellis

TOMÁS TÓIBÍN

Tomás Tóibín was born in Cork in 1920. A poet, teacher and civil servant, he has translated a number of French, German and Spanish plays into Irish, and Gogol's *Inspector General* from the Russian. His first collection, *Súil le Cuan* (1967), received an Arts Council Award in 1968. His second, *Duilliúr*, was published in 1983.

An Taispeántas An Uile

Is fónta ann féin an t-éadach is an t-eolas,
is le stuacacht airím airgead chomh maith.
Tá trasnálaithe róchéillí a bhréagnódh mé
ach den uain seo is agamsa atá an ceart!

Ní fóntacht síoda is cás le bean an ghúna
    ámh,
ná ceardúlacht na maintíne, dá
    fheabhas,
ach stróinsí fir ag stánadh uirthi á iompar
is fearmad ban ná sealbhaíonn a shamhail.

Ní taise puinn don eolach: ní sprionlóir é
ná chaithfeadh ór an léinn—breá leis é roinnt.
Ní foghlaim, ach a ghradam inti, is glóir leis.
Chun scaipithe a chruinníonn saoi, chun céime a
    shaint.

The Display is Everything

Clothing and knowledge are good in themselves,
I stubbornly reckon money is also.
Over-sensible hecklers will contradict me,
But on this occasion it is I who am right.

The quality of the silk does not trouble
	the lady in the gown however,
Nor does the craftsmanship of the seamstress
	however excellent,
But the eyes of strange men upon her wearing it,
and the envy of women who do not own the like.

The professor is just the same: he's not a miser
who will not spend the gold of learning—he
	enjoys sharing it.
He glories not in learning, but in his distinction in it,
The learned man gathers to scatter, he covets honour.

'Nocht an dollar',
a deir an Poncánach.
Ní olc an tOllamh é
i leith an Taispeántais.

An Paisinéir Eile

Hata seicear air is cleitín . . .
Cóta dufail 's bróga svaeide,
'Na chlab bhí píopa cam aige
'Gus dhá sciathán croiméil air.
Ba chatsúileach mo bhreithniú
Is mheás dom féin a thréithe.

    Dhaoras é im aigne
    (Gan caidreamh leis in aon chor)
    A ionannú le haicme fear
    Lér beag gach ní dá ngéillim.
    Ceapann gach aon amadán
    Gurb é féin fear na léire.

Dá mbeadh clóca gan uaim air,
Dá mba chamall-rón a léine
Dá mbeadh dealga mar hata air,
Is mise i measc an daoscair,
An mbeinn ag fógairt croise air
Gan caidreamh leis in aon chor?

'Flash the dollar',
So says the Yank.
He's no bad expert
On these pranks.

Translated by Pádraig Mac Fhearghusa

The Other Passenger

Chequered hat and little feather . . .
Duffle coat and suede shoes,
He had a crooked pipe in his mouth,
And had two wings of a moustache.
My adjudication was a catlike glance,
And I weighed for myself his qualities.

I condemned him in my mind
(Without any social intercourse with him)
Identifying him with a class of men
Who think little of all in which I believe.
Every fool thinks
That he himself is the man of clarity.

If he had worn a seamless cloak,
If his shirt were of camel-hair,
If there were thorns as a hat upon him,
And I among the mob,
Would I have been threatening him with crucifixion,
Without ever knowing him?

Translated by Pádraig Mac Fhearghusa

MÁIRE MHAC AN tSAOI

Máire Mhac an tSaoi was born in Dublin in 1922. Educated at University College, Dublin and at the Sorbonne. She served as a diplomat with the Irish Department of Foreign Affairs. She worked on the preparation of the *English-Irish Dictionary*. She married Conor Cruise O'Brien in 1962 and lived for several years in Ghana and New York before returning to Ireland to live in Howth.

Fógra

Ógánaigh sin an cheana, dá dtuigtheá tú féin i
 gceart
Bhraithfeá an bhliain ag caitheamh is na laethanta ag
 imeacht;
Leat, an fhaid a mhairfidh, an luisne sin i
 gcneas,
An bláth san ar an leacain, an tathaint sin na
 ndearc,
Ach ní mór don taoide casadh, is sé dán na hoíche
 teacht.

Chím chughat an tuar ins an uair ná haithneofar
Breáthacht do chlúimhse thar ghearrcaigh na
 gcomharsan,
Mustar do chúrsa i gcuibhreann ban óg duit,
Crot an chinn chúmtha, ná guaille atá córach
Crochta go huaibhreach fén seanachasóig sin.

Warning

And oh! young man so coaxing, if you'd but think
    again,
You'd know the year was wasting and the long days
    drawing in;
The glow that lights your face there, before the turn
    of tide,
Is yours now, that entreaty, that bloom, those
    speaking eyes,
But the night comes on apace, boy, and these things
    don't abide.

When they confuse them—and I see it threaten—
Neighbour child's plumage with your splendid
    feathers:
Comely head lifted on shapely shoulder,
High-carried proudly above that old coat, lad,
And among maidens your effortless boasting . . .

Fair tú féin is seachain, ós tú an tarna mac,
Sara dtagthá turas abhaile is ná beadh romhat cead
    isteach,
Is áilleachtaí do phearsan ná fóirfeadh ort, nár
    chleacht
Suáilce fós ná carthain is réim an tsrutha leat—
Nuair a theipeann ar an dtaitneamh is tarcaisneach a
    bhlas.

Cluas dom, a dhalta, is meabhraigh an méid seo,
Is má luír do shúil ar chailín i leith chughat ina
    dhéidh seo
Ná dein iontas de ná tagann: ba leor uait uair an
    sméideadh
Ach anois tá dulta amach ort, is do tugadh ort do
    thréithe,
Is mo thrua í mar a mealladh, más miste thú le
    héinne.

Watch yourself, be wary, for you're the second son,
And one day you'll come home again and they'll not
    let you in—
The beauties of your person will leave you stranded
    dry
Who never practised decency when you were riding
    high—
When inclination fails, the taste is bitter eating, boy!

Hark to me, neighbour, bear this much in mind:
When next you're wishful to convey that you're to
    dance inclined
And girls don't rise and come your way, don't you be
    too surprised—
There was a time a wink would do, but now they're
    all apprised—
And some there be who pity you, but few, boy, and
    not I!

Translated by the author

Ceathrúintí Mháire Ní Ógáin

1

Ach a mbead gafa as an líon so—
Is nár lige Dia gur fada san—
Béidir go bhfónfaidh cuimhneamh
Ar a bhfuaireas de shuaimhneas id bhaclainn.

Nuair a bheidh ar mo chumas guíochtaint,
Comaoine is éisteacht Aifrinn,
Cé déarfaidh ansan nach cuí dhom
Ar 'shonsa is ar mo shon féin achaine?

Ach comhairle idir dhá linn duit,
Ná téir ródhílis in achrann,
Mar go bhfuilimse meáite ar scaoileadh
Pé cuibhrinn a snaidhmfear eadrainn.

ll

Beagbheann ar amhras daoine,
Beagbheann ar chros na sagart,
Ar gach ní ach bheith sínte
Idir tú agus falla—

Neamhshuím liom fuacht na hoíche,
Neamhshuím liom scríb is fearthainn,
Sa domhan cúng rúin teolaí seo
Ná téann thar fhaobhar na leapan—

Ar a bhfuil romhainn ní smaoinfeam,
Ar a bhfuil déanta cheana,
Linne an uain, a chroí istigh,
Is mairfidh sí go maidin.

Quatrains of Mary Hogan

1

Once I am rid of these meshes—
God send it be soon and forever!
It may not be counted unseemly
My peace in your arms to remember.

When prayer becomes possible to me,
With Mass and receipt of Communion,
Oh, who will declare it indecent
To entreat for myself or for you, love?

But, while we await this conclusion,
Do not grow too deeply enamoured,
For I am committed to loosing
All bonds that could ever be fastened. ←—

Net → affair?
body?

11

All ban of priest defying,
Indifferent to all
Suspicion, I am lying
Between you and the wall.

Night's winter weather cannot
Reach here to change my mind—
Warm, secret world and narrow,
Within one bed confined;

What is to come we heed not,
Nor what was done before,
The time is ours, my dearest,
And it will last till dawn.

III

Achar bliana atáim
Ag luí farat id chlúid,
Deacair anois a rá
Cad leis a raibh mo shúil!

Ghabhais de chosaibh i gcion
A tugadh go fial ar dtúis,
Gan aithint féin féd throigh
Fulaing na feola a bhrúigh!

Is fós tá an creat umhal
Ar mhaithe le seanagheallúint,
Ach ó thost cantain an chroí
Tránn áthas an phléisiúir.

IV

Tá naí an éada ag deol mo chí'se
Is mé ag tál air de ló is d'oíche;
An gárlach gránna ag cur na bhfiacal,
Is de nimh a ghreama mo chuisle líonta

A ghrá, ná maireadh an trú beag eadrainn,
Is a fholláine, shláine a bhí ár n-aithne;
Barántas cnis a chlóigh lem chneas airsin,
Is séala láimhe a raibh gach cead aici.

Féach nach meáite mé ar chion a shéanadh,
Cé gur sháigh an t-amhras go doimhin a phréa'cha;
Ar láir dhea-tharraic ná déan éigean,
Is díolfaidh sí an comhar leat ina shéasúr féinig.

lll

So we must reckon a year
That we the one coverlet share,
Difficult now to be clear
What I wanted, for what came prepared?

Mine was a generous love—
You trampled it under your heel—
With never a question at all
If the flesh that was trodden could feel?

Oh, but the body obeys,
For the sake of a long-given word,
But now that the song in the heart has been stayed
Joy ebbs from our pleasure like tide on the turn.

IV

Infant jealousy feeds at my breast:
I must nurse by day, I must nurse by night;
He's an ugly youngster and teething fast,
And he poisons my veins with his milk-tooth bite.

Don't let the small wretch separate us—
So sound and healthy as was our mating!
Its warrant was skin to skin that clave, and
Its seal a hand granted every favour.

I have no mind to deny affection
Though doubt takes root in deep dejection—
Do not abuse a good draft mare then,
And she, in her own time, will repair all.

V

Is éachtach an rud í an phian,
Mar chaitheann an cliabh,
Is ná tugann faoiseamh ná spás
Ná sánas de ló ná d'oích'—

An té atá i bpéin mar táim
Ní raibh uaigneach ná ina aonar riamh,
Ach ag iompar cuileachtan de shíor
Mar bhean gin féna coim.

VI

'Ní chodlaím ist oíche'—
Beag an rá, ach an bhfionnfar
        choíche
Ar shúile oscailte
Ualach na hoíche?

VII

Fada liom anocht!
Do bhí ann oíche
Nárbh fhada faratsa—
Dá leomhfainn cuimhneamh.

Go deimhin níor dheacair san,
An ród a d'fhillfinn—
Dá mba cheadaithe
Tar éis aithrí ann.

Luí chun suilt
Is éirí chun aoibhnis
Siúd ba chleachtadh dhúinn—
Dá bhfaighinn dul siar air.

V

Oh, what a wonder is pain!
How it gnaws at the cage
Of the ribs! And it will not abate
Or be sated, come night or come day.

Thus it is, pain is made known,
You will never be sole or alone,
But will carry your company close
Like a mother her babe in the womb.

VI

'I do not sleep of nights':
It is not much to say,
But who has yet devised a way to calculate,
Upon the open eye,
How heavy the night's weight.

VII

The night is long!
There were nights once
With you not long—
Which I renounce.

Not hard to follow
The road I want;
No longer possible
If I repent.

We lay for mirth
And we rose with gladness—
Practices such
As I must abandon.   *Translated by the author*

Note: Mary Hogan, the mistress of the eighteenth century poet Donncha Rua
Mac Conmara, is the archetype of the unhappy female lover in Irish folklore.

Sunt Lacrimae Rerum
I nDilchuimhne ar Shéamus Ennis

Sianaíl ag síofraí, geimhreata an gheon;
Caoighol ag símhná i bhfogus is fós
Siar go roinn duimhche: a Dhionn, scaoil an sceol.

Súiste í uaill an droma mhóir—
    Tarraing go tréan;
Dlúigh le gach buille ina chóir,
    Tuargan an léin;
Taoiseach, iarn' ídeach don gceol,
    Gabhann chun an chré.

Ruaig ar lucht leasa agus brogha, mashlua an aeir;
Gruagaigh na scairte i luísheol, chucu an chíréip;
Grianáras Aonghusa ar Bóinn spéirling do réab.

Fásach gan cláirseach
    Fad tharla an Teamhair 'na féar;
Go hanois áfach
    Téarnamh ón léan
Níor chuaidh dar n-áireamh—
    Feasta tám tréith.

Tocht broinne an aithrígh bheir bláth ar bhachall
    droighin;
De shians chroit Oirféis, an gallán cloiche rinnc;
Ach, a ríphíobaire Eireann, clos duit ní dán arís—
                Choíche!

Lament

For Séamus Ennis, Late Champion Piper of Ireland   (Slow Air)

Sheepeople wheening, wintry their wail;
Fairy wives keening near and away
West to the dune's edge: Donn [1], spread the tale.

Make the drum's roar a flail—
    Lay on great strokes,
Redoubling each in train,
    Hammers of woe;
This prince, the music waned,
    Seeks his clay home.

Wizards of liss and fort, hosts of the air,
Panicked and routed go, each from his lair;
Boyne's [2] airy pleasure-dome, rainstorm lays bare.

Desert and harpless,
    Tara is grass;
Yet we had argued
    Even such pass
No mortal harm meant—
    No more, alas!

White flowers of repentance the barren staff
    knew;
The pillar-stones danced to hear Orpheus' tunes;
But, King-piper of Ireland, voice is witheld from you—
                  Ever!

Translation (elaborated from a first draft by Canon Coslett Quinn) by the author.

[1]   *Donn duimhche*, 'Donn of the Dune', was the old Irish god of death
[2]   The prehistoric tombs on the Boyne were believed to be the palaces of the old gods.

Codladh an Ghaiscígh

Ceannín mogallach milis mar sméar—
A mhaicín iasachta, a chuid den tsaoil,
Dé do bheathasa is neadaigh im chroí,
Dé do bheathasa fé fhrathacha an tí,
A réilthín maidine 'tháinig i gcéin.

Is maith folaíocht isteach!
Féach mo bhullán beag d'fhear:
Sáraigh da doras é nó ceap
I dtubán—Chomh folláin le breac
Gabhaimse orm! Is gach ball fé rath,
An áilleacht mar bharr ar an neart—

Do thugais ón bhfómhar do dhath
Is ón rós crón. Is deas
Gach buí óna chóngas leat.
Féach, a Chonchúir, ár mac,
Ní mar beartaíodh ach mar cheap
Na cumhachta in airde é 'theacht.

Tair go dtím' bachlainn, a chircín eornan,
Tá an lampa ar lasadh is an oíche ag tórmach,
Tá an mada rua ag siúl an bóthar,
Nár sheola aon chat mara ag snapadh é id threosa,
Nuair gur coinneal an teaghlaigh ar choinnleoirín
    óir tú.

The Hero's Sleep

Blackberry-sweet, the little clustered head!
Small foreign son, my share of this world's treasure,
Nest and be welcome underneath my heart;
Nest and be welcome underneath our rafters;
You've come a long way, little morning star.

It is good so to breed, from without:
See my manling, my little bull-calf—
Head him off from the door, trap him safe in his bath—
On my word, he's as sound as a trout,
In every limb prospering stoutly,
In strength, and in beauty to crown it.

You took your colour from the Autumn
And from the dun rose:
Lovely all yellows! They are your relations—
Look, Conor, here then our son,
Not as his advent was planned,
But as Providence put it in hand.

My small barley hen, let me gather you in;
The night's darkness threatens, the lamp has been lit;
The fox is abroad on the roads—
No ill-hap send him snapping to our door,
Where you shine, the household's candle, on a candle-
    stick of gold!

Id shuan duit fém' borlach
Is fál umat mo ghean—
Ar do chamachuaird má sea
Fuar agam bheith dhed' bhrath.
Cén chosaint a bhéarfair leat?
Artha? Leabharúin? Nó geas?
'Ná taobhaigh choíche an geal,'
Paidir do chine le ceart.

Ar nós gach máthar seal
Deinim mo mhachnamh thart
Is le linn an mheabhraithe
Siúd spíonóig mhaide id ghlaic!
Taibhrítear dom go pras
An luan láich os do chneas
I leith is gur chugham a bheadh,
Garsúinín Eamhna, Cú na gCleas!

Asleep beneath my breast
My love has walled you in,
But when your kingly steps go forth,
I dog your path in vain.
What charm will keep you safe?
What talisman prevail?
Is not 'No treaty with the white!'
Your proper tribal prayer?

As is a mother's way,
I let my thoughts run on,
And while my mind debates,
You've seized the wooden spoon!
At once my dream is changed,
Your hero's light shines round—
Just such another little boy,
They say, was Ulster's Hound.

Translated by the author

Fómhar Na Farraige

Sheo linn ar thórramh an Gharlaigh Choileánaigh
Is i ndoras an tseomra bhí romhainn an mháithrín,
'A mhaicín ó,' ar sí, 'Ní raibh críne i ndán duit
Is is dual don óige bheith fiáin rascánta—
Is ochón!' . . .

Fíoghar ar mo shúile iad cneácha míofara a mic,
Is snagaíl fhiata a ghlórtha is teinn trém chluasaibh—
An gearrcach gránna an dá uair báite againn,
Greas insa t-srúill is greas fén mbladar tomtha—
Is ochón!

Lasann 'na ghnúis chugham an dá shméaróid dhóite;
Rian na gcúig mhéar mo leiceadarsa 'tharraing
Tráth gabhadh é is a ladhar aige sa
        phróca . . .
Is duitse atáim á insint, a phoill an fhalla!
Is ochón!

'gCloistí an mháthair? 'Fé mar chaith sé liomsa!
Is tar éis gur fhág príosún d'fhill ar an bhfaoistin' . . .
Do scar an mhrúch a folt glas-uaithne ar Chonaing—
D'fhuadaigh ó fhód na croiche an cincíseach!
Is ochón!

Amhantarán ón gceallúraigh in' aithbhreith
Ag sianaíl choíche ar rian na daonnachta!
Iarlais ins a' tsíog gaoithe ar neamhmbeith!
Coillteán na trua ón aithis dhéanach so!
Is ochón!

Harvest of the Sea

We set off to the wake of our graceless neighbour—
In the bedroom stood his Mammy waiting—
'O little son,' she said, 'Age was not your portion,
And youth is wont to be wild and rakish—
And ochone!' . . .

My sight retains his unattractive features,
His nagging, eerie whine aches through my hearing—
Drown we the scaldy bastard yet again then:
Once in the tide-race, now in adulation—
And ochone!

I've seen those eyes there, fiery, like embers burning,
Track of five fingers my slap drew across them,
Who caught him with his fist wedged in the crock-
    mouth—
Hole in the wall, to you I tell my burden—
And ochone!

Hark to the mother, 'How he treated me, though!
And after he left gaol, went to confession!'
The sea-wife's blue-green hair spread over Conaing,[1]
Wrapt from the gallows-foot the Whitsun weanling[2]—
And ochone!

Unbaptised, reincarnate by mistake,
Coveting human substance, ever wailing,
In fairy wind annihilated, changeling,
And still insulted, pitiful, castrated—
And ochone!

Ná bí ag brath ormsa, 'ainniseoir!
Id cháilíocht fhéin dob ann duit dá shuaraí í—
Ach ní réitíonn an marbh is an beo
Hook your own ground! Ní mise bard do
    chaointe—
Is ochón! . . .

Éignigh a ghreim den ngunail—bíodh acu!
Cuir suas an t-íomhá céireach i measc na gcoinneal,
An féinics gléasta tar éis a thonachtha,
Is téadh an giobal scéite síos go grinneall—
Is ochón! . . .

Scéal uaim ar thórramh an Gharlaigh
    Choileánaigh,
Níor facathas fós dúinn aon tsochraid chomh breá
    léi,
Cliar agus tuath is an dubh ina bhán ann—
Is bearna a' mhíl i bhfolach fén gclár ann!
Is ochón!

Do not depend on me, wretch, don't come near me—
In your own right, though sordid, you existed—
But dead and living do not suit together—
'Hook your own ground!' I'm not the bard to keen
        you—
And ochone!

Force his grip from the gunwale—let them win!
Put up the waxen image—light the candles—
Phoenix arrayed after his death-washing!
And let the spent rag sink to the sea-bottom—
And ochone!

Tell the tale, how they waked him, the graceless
        youngster—
Faith, the funeral they gave him was surely a
        wonder—
Black was made white there, by clergy and laymen,
And the coffin-lid covered, for ever, the hare-lip—
And ochone!

Translated by the author

Oíche Nollag

Le coinnle na n-aingeal tá an spéir amuigh breactha,
Tá fiacail an tseaca sa ghaoith ón gcnoc,
Adaigh an tine is téir chun na leapan,
Luífidh Mac Dé ins an tigh seo anocht.

Fágaidh an doras ar leathadh ina coinne,
An mhaighdean a thiocfaidh is a naí ar a hucht,
Deonaigh do shuaimhneas a ligint, a Mhuire,
Luíodh Mac Dé ins an tigh seo anocht.

Bhí soilse ar lasadh i dtigh sin na haíochta,
Cóiriú gan caoile, bia agus deoch,
Do cheannaithe olla, do cheannaithe síoda,
Ach luífidh Mac Dé ins an tigh seo anocht.

Christmas Eve

With candles of angels the sky is now dappled,
The frost on the wind from the hills has a bite,
Kindle the fire and go to your slumber
Jesus will lie in this household tonight.

Leave all the doors wide open before her,
The Virgin who'll come with the child on her breast,
Grant that you'll stop here tonight, Holy Mary,
That Jesus tonight in this household may rest.

The lights were all lighting in that little hostel,
There were generous servings of victuals and wine
For merchants of silk, for merchants of woollens,
But Jesus will lie in this household tonight.

Translated by Gabriel Fitzmaurice

BREANDÁN Ó BEACHÁIN

Breandán Ó Beacháin (Brendan Behan) was born in Dublin in 1923. Internationally renowned for his work in the English language, he published poems in Irish in various periodicals. At the invitation of Gael Linn, he wrote a play in Irish, *An Giall*, which he later translated as *The Hostage*. He was the youngest contributor to Seán Ó Tuama's anthology, *Nuabhéarsaíocht* (1950). He died in Dublin in 1964.

Uaigneas

Blas sméara dubh'
tréis báisteach
ar bharr an tsléibhe.

I dtost an phríosúin
Feadaoil fhuar na traenach.

Cogar gáire beirt leannán
don aonarán.

Loneliness   imagistic

The blackberries' taste
after rainfall
on the hilltop.

In the silence of prison
the train's cold whistle.

The whisper of laughing lovers
to the lonely.

Translated by Ulick O'Connor

Oscar Wilde
Do Shéan O Súilleabháin

*Oscar Wilde, Poète et Dramaturge, né à Dublin le 15 octobre,
1856, est mort dans cette maison le 30 novembre, 1900.*

Tar éis gach gleo
do chuir sé as beo
le teann anaithe,
sínte san chlapsholus
corpán an bheomhaire
balbh san dorchadas.
Fé thost, ach coinnle
an tórraimh na lasracha.
A cholainn sheang
's a shúil daingean ídithe
i seomra fuar lom
's an *concierge* spídeach
ó an iomarca freastail
ar phótaire iasachta
a d'imthigh gan service
an deich fén gcéad íoctha.
Aistrith' ón Flore
do fhásach na naomhthacht,
ógphrionnsa na bpeacadh
ina shearbhán aosta,
seod órdha na drúise
ina dhiaidh aige fághta,
gan *Pernod* ina chabhair aige
ach uisce na cráifeacht.
ógrí na háilleacht
ina Narcissus briste,
ach réalt na glanmhaighdine
ina ga ar an uisce.

Oscar Wilde
To Sean O'Sullivan

Oscar Wilde, Poète et Dramaturge, né à Dublin le 15 octobre, 1856, est mort dans cette maison le 30 novembre, 1900.

After all the wit
in a sudden fit
of fear, he skipped it.
Stretched in the twilight
that body once lively
dumb in the darkness.
In a cold empty room
quiet, but for candles
blazing beside him,
his elegant form
and firm gaze exhausted.
With a spiteful concierge
impatient at waiting
for a foreign waster
who left without paying
the ten per cent service.
Exiled now from Flore
to sanctity's desert
the young prince of Sin
broken and withered.
Lust left behind him
gem without lustre
no Pernod for a stiffner
but cold holy water
the young king of beauty
Narcissus broken.
But the pure star of Mary
as a gleam on the ocean.

Ceangal

Dá aoibhne bealach an pheacaidh
is mairg bás gan beannacht
Mo ghraidhn thú, a Oscair,
bhí sé agat gach bealach.

Guidhe An Rannaire

Dá bhfeicinn fear fásta, as Gaoluinn líofa,
Ag cur síos go síbhialta ar nithe 's ar dhaoine,
Meon is tuairimí i ráite an lae seo,
Soibealta, sómhar, soicheallach, saolta
—Bheinn an-shásta a theagasc d'éisteacht.
File fiáin, fearúil, feadánach
Bard beo bíoghach bríomhar bastallach
Pianta paiseanta peannphágánach.

Ariú, mo chreach, cad é an fhírinne?
Stát-sheirbhísigh ó Chorca Dhuibhne,
Bobarúin eile ó chladaigh Thír Chonaill
'S ó phortaigh na Gaillimh' mar bharr ar an ndonas,
Gaeil Bhleá Cliath na n-órchnap fáinne,
Pioneers páistiúla, pollta, piteánta,
Maighdeana malla maola marfánta
Gach duine acu críochnaithe cúramach, cráifeach.

Dá dtiocfadh file ag séideadh gríosaí
Raghainn abhaile, mo ghnó agam críochnaíth'.

Envoi

Sweet is the way of the sinner,
sad, death without God's praise.
My life on you, Oscar boy,
yourself had it both ways.

Translated by Ulick O'Connor

The Versemaker's Wish   *Irish revival*

If I saw a fine fellow with fluent Irish
Civilly spouting on deeds and people
In our own language, a marvellous earful,
Cocky, comfortable, casual, cheerful,
I'd be well pleased to pay attention;
Passionate poet, proud, productive,
Brave bard, brisk bouncing buccaneer,
Pleasant, pagan-penned, perceptive.

Alas, alack, what is my story?
Civil Servants from Corcauguiney
Other eejits from Donegal foreshore,
Clodhoppers from Galway to make my head sore.
Dublin gaels afflicted with fáinnes
Puerile pioneers,[1] pansified and punctured,
Vacant virgins, vehement and vulgar.
All dedicated to prudence and piety.

If a poet came to stir these embers
I'd leave for home my task accomplished.

Translated by Ulick O'Connor

[1] A Pioneer in Ireland is commonly taken to mean a member of an organisation who
takes a religious vow to abstain for life from alcohol

L'Existentialisme
(Macalla St Germain-de-Prés)

A fhir faire, tá ag siúl falla—
foirgnimh falaimh.
Cad is cúrsa na seilge?
cúis reilge.
Turas go hifreann?
Ní foláir, céard fé d'intinn?
Cad a bhí ann romhainn?
Ní fios, ní rabhas beo,
nílim fós.
Olc ár gciniúint?
ró-leisciúil,
freagra thabhairt.
Maitheas, níl a dhath,
ná ciall ná pian, fiú amháin,
ná an fhírinne im'abairt—
ná 'na mhalairt.

L'Existentialisme
(An echo of St Germain-de-Prés)

Watchmen on the wall patrolling
your empty building
how is the hunt going,
the graveyard doing,
is our voyage to hell?
Must be! Is your mind well?
What went before us, tell?
Don't know; I was not alive
I am not, yet
is our fate stinking?
too lazy
to answer that one.
Good: there's not a bit
of sense or pain, still less
truth, in what I say
or in the opposite way.

Translated by Ulick O'Connor

Buíochas Le Joyce

Anseo i *Rue Saint André des Arts*
I dtábhairne Arabach, ólta,
Míním do Fhrancach fiosrach thú
Do *ex-G.I.'s* is do Rúiseach ólta.
Molaim gach comhartha dár chuiris ar phár
Is mise sa Fhrainc ag ól *Pernod* dá bharr,
Maidir le *conteur*, is bródúil sinn asat
Is buíoch den *Calvados* ólaimid tríot.

Dá mba mise tusa
Is tusa mé féin
Ag teacht ó *Les Halles*
Is ag iompar an méid seo *cognac*
Ag seinm ar lánbholg
Scríobhfása véarsa nó dhó do mo mholadh!

Gratitude to James Joyce

Here in the rue St André des Arts,
Plastered in an Arab Tavern,
I explain you to an eager Frenchman,
Ex-GI's and a drunken Russian,
Of all you wrote I explain each part,
Drinking Pernod in France because of your art.
As a writer we're proud of you—
And thanks for the Calvados we gain through you.

If I were you
And you were me,
Coming from Les Halles
Roaring, with a load of cognac,
Belly full, on the tipple,
A verse or two in my honour you'd scribble.

Translated by Ulick O'Connor

Jackeen Ag Caoineadh Na mBlascaod
Do Sheán Ó Briain as Baile an Fheirtéaraigh

Beidh an fharraige mhór faoi luí gréine mar ghloine,
Gan bád faoi sheol ná comhartha beo ó dhuine
Ach an t-iolar órga deireanach thuas ar
     imeall
An domhain, thar an mBlascaod uaigneach luite . . .

An ghrian ina luí is scáth na hoíche á scaipeadh
Ar ardú ré is í ag taitneamh i bhfuacht trí
     scamaill,
A méara loma sínte síos ar thalamh
Ar thithe scriosta briste, truamhar folamh . . .

Faoi thost ach cleití na n-éan ag cuimilt thar tonna
Buíoch as a bheith fillte, ceann i mbrollach faoi
     shonas,
Séideadh na gaoithe ag luascadh go bog leathdhorais
Is an teallach fuar fliuch, gan tine, gan teas, gan
     chosaint.

A Jackeen[1] Says Goodbye to the Blaskets

The great sea under the setting sun gleams like a glass,
Not a sail in sight, no living person to see it pass
Save the last golden eagle, hung on the edge of the
    world,
Over the lonely Blasket resting, his wings unfurled.

Yes, the sun's at rest now and shadows thicken the
    light,
A rising moon gleams coldly through the night,
Stretching thin fingers down the quivering air,
On desolate, deserted dwellings, pitifully bare.

Silent save for birds' wings clipping the foam,
Heads on breast, they rest content, grateful to be
    home.
The wind lifts lightly, setting the half-door aslope,
On a famished hearth without heat, without
    protection, without hope.

Translated by Ulick O'Connor

1 Jackeen: The Irish Countryman's name for a Dubliner

EITHNE STRONG

Eithne Strong was born in 1923 in Glensharrold, Co. Limerick. In 1943 she married Rupert Strong, poet and psychoanalyst, who died in 1984. A teacher, broadcaster, poet and short-story writer in both Irish and English, her collections of poems include *Songs of the Living* (1961) and *Sarah in Passing* (1974), a novel *Degrees of Kindred* (1979), *Flesh ... The Greatest Sin*, a long poem first published in 1980, and a collection of short stories, *Patterns* (1981). Her first collection of Irish poetry *Cirt Oibre* was published in 1974 and a second, *Fuil agus Fallaí* in 1983. *My Darling Neighbour* was published in 1985. *Aoife Faoi Ghlas*, a collection in Irish, and another volume in English were published in 1989.

Mar A Fuarthas Spreagadh
[As *An Scread* le hEdvard Munch]

Féach
mo thacaíocht mheánaicmeach
—ní háil liom ganntanas—
eagar is ord mo thí
—cracálaí is fuath liom—
éirim is slacht mo mhéin
—is gráin liom óinseach—

Ach
deich n-uaire in aghaidh an lae
ionsaím dún na céille; compord
an oird scriosaim as alt;
maise na seascaire, loitim í;
pléascaim an dlús teolaí:
is gealt os íseal mé.

Response to Munch's *Scream*

See
my middle-class bastions
—scarcity I detest;
the order and method of my house
—I abominate a scatterbrain;
decorum and reserve my manner
—one abhors gush.

But
ten times a day
I assail the walls of sanity
tear comfort raw
slash at padded ease
wreck the engulfing cloy.
Secretly I am a lunatic.

111

Éist
is éigean dom réabadh san uaigneas,
dualgas an gheilt 'chur i gcion
thar ghnácht an ghnáis,
scéird-bhrú na mire 'chomlíonadh
—cuibhreann na huaighe am thachtadh san só:
an scread rosc catha mo shaoirse.

Hear
I must shatter the void
rend to maniac necessity
beyond the stale of habit
burst to crazy power:
comfort chokes in muffling tyranny
the scream is my survival.

Translated by Eithne Strong

SEÁN Ó TUAMA

Seán Ó Tuama was born in Cork in 1926. As Professor of Irish Language and Culture at University College Cork, he lectured extensively in American, English and French Universities. Poet, playwright and editor, his anthology, *An Duanaire: 1600-1900 Poems of the Dispossessed* (1981) with Thomas Kinsella, introduced the poetry in Irish of that period to a new and wider audience.

Cá Siúlfam?

Cá siúlfam? Tá na cosáin reoite,
carnáin chalcaithe de shneachta cruaite
ar bhlaincéadaí ar bhóthair mar a mbíodh ár siúl.
'S tá an ghaoth ag aimsiú ioscada na nglún
chomh géar chomh glic le fuip . . .
Ní shiúlfad leat. Tá an corp ina chloch.

Tiomáinfeam? Racham ar an aifreann déanach
ag éisteacht le Hosanna in Excelsis
á ghreadadh amach go buach caithréimeach,
is bainfeam sásamh as an at gan éifeacht
a thagann ar an gcroí . . .
Chauffeur mé, lá seaca, ar dheabhóidí.

Ar deireadh: ní chorródsa amach inniu,
tá fuil i gcúl mo bhéil le mí ón sioc,
is ó inchinn go talamh síos
tá bánú déanta ar gach artaire
a dhéanann duine den daonaí . . .
Fanfam féach an bhfillfidh teas arís.

Where shall we Walk?

Where shall we walk? The paths are all iced over,
on the grassy blankets of the roads we've known
calcified mounds of slush and snow,
the wind stings the hollows of the knees
as slyly and as sharply as a whip . . .
I shall not walk with you. The flesh is stone.

We shall drive then, go to Mass,
listen to Hosanna in Excelsis
being ground out triumphally,
and feed upon the silly satisfaction
of music swelling up the heart . . .
On a frosty day I act as chauffeur to the mysteries.

No, just no: I will not move today
the chill has bloodied up my throat this long month past,
and every artery that makes a human burn
from brain down to the ground
has been whitened to debility . . .
We'll wait and see if heat returns.

Translated by the author

An File Dá Bhean
[as an dráma *Corp Eoghain Uí Shúilleabháin*]

Oíche lán de cheatha beaga ar dhúiseacht dom,
casaim chughat is chím le léire iontasach
gur strainséar coirp tú sínte síos le sliasaid liom,
is áthasaíonn an t-ainmhí istigh ionam.

Ach sé dúrt liom féin aréir 's an spéir amuigh á scoil
(is an t-ainmhí simplí istigh faoi scanradh ionam):
'dá bhfaighfeá bás anois
do leaghfadh náire mé.'
Níl ansin adeir mo chiall inniu le gaois
ach seana-nath gan bhrí.
Cuireann an duine daonna de formhór gach ní . . .

Fós, thuig mo chroí aréir gur náire follasach
nár mhó ná strainséar riamh bhí liom chun cónaithe
gur lú tar éis na mblian mo thuiscint ort,
ná ar athair is deartháir is daoine muinteartha
nár mhalartaíos sa tsaol seo riamh ach focail leo.
'Níor mhaite d'éinne' (adúrt), 'faillí chomh coirpeac
    san!'

Ach gan mhoill 'na dhiaidh sin scoir na toirneacha
    amuigh,
is bhís chomh te teolaí, strainséartha, lán de chion,
gur áthasaigh an t-ainmhí arís istigh ionam.

The Poet to his Wife

[From a three-act play *Four Cheers for Cremation*]

A night of light persistent showers when I awake,
I turn towards you and see in wonderment
a stranger, motionless, laid out by my side,
and the animal within me leaps, elatedly.

But last night as thunder split the sky
(and the animal within cowed low in misery)
I said, 'If you, my wife this moment died
shame would melt my heart and limbs.'
Today, of course, my reason jibs
at cosmic clichés of the kind.
A human being, I know, survives most things.

Yet, last night, my heart realised the melting shame
of having kept you as a stranger in my territory,
someone who after all those years I know much less
than father, mother, brothers, relatives—
who in this life exchange but words with me.
'Neglect like this,' I told myself, 'is bred out of
         barbarity.'

But when the rumble in the sky had lost its potency,
and you my stranger wife beside me, soft and full of
         tenderness,
the animal in me leaped up again for ectasy.

Translated by the author

Besides, Who Knows Before the End, What Light May Shine

Maidin ghorm ins an Ghréig
(an leathchéad scoite agam)
faoi bhíomaí buí is giolcaigh fhite—
mo chorp ar teitheadh ón ngréin.

Liszt go glinn im chluais ag cumasc
le lapaíl shámh na dtonn,
táim síoraí anseo sa bhfuarthan
idir fallaí bána an tí.

An túisce stopann an pianó
tránn an mhuir fém chroí,
is cuimhním ar dhaoine age baile
a bhí mór im chathair tráth.

Ceathrar fear im chathairse
a éiríonn romham sa tost,
an luisne ard do mhúscail siad
do dheineas cimilt léi.

An saoi a chrith le gile an tsolais
i gceartain seanfhilí,
an draoi scaoil caisí ceoil thar cora—
is a bháigh é féin sa tsruth.

An file cráite a mhúnlaigh nua—
scamhóga Gaeilge dúinn,
an dealbhadóir chuir clocha ag rince
lena sheanchaíocht.

Besides, Who Knows Before the End, What Light May Shine

A blue mid-morning here in Greece
(my fiftieth year passed by),
under mottled beams and woven reeds—
body flees from sun.

Liszt, lucid in my ears, is merging
with the soft lap of the waves,
I'm immortal in this coolness,
enclosed between white walls.

As soon as the piano ceases
the sea ebbs from my heart
and I think of people home in my city
who, not long ago, stood high.

Four men from my native city
rise before me now,
the glow of mind which they created
I rubbed against a while:

a sage who trembled at the brightness
in the forge of ancient poets,
a druid who released our damned-up music
and perished in the flood,

a tortured poet who fashioned for us
new Irish-language lungs,
a sculptor who set headstones dancing
with his carefree lore.

File, ceoltóir, dealbhadóir,
is rompu an máistir-saoi,
ina measc siúd do tharlaíos-sa;
ní tharlóidh sé arís.

Maidin ghorm ins an Ghréig
(an leathchéad scoite agam)
ag cuimhneamh ar an luisne a bhí—
is cúrsa é roimh bás.

Anois an t-am don rince aonair
ar ghainimh bheo na trá—
na cosa a chaitheamh go háiféiseach
is leá d'aonghnó sa teas.

Musician, poet and sculptor,
and before them master-sage,
I happened to occur amongst them,
it will not occur again.

A blue mid-morning here in Greece
(my fiftieth year passed by)
thinking of the glow that was—
that's matter for the dying.

Better rise up now, a solo-dancer,
on the hot sands of the strand,
throw out both legs, at random,
and melt down in the sun.

Translated by the author

PEARSE HUTCHINSON

Pearse Hutchinson was born in Glasgow in 1927 of Irish parents, and reared in Dublin from 1932. Poet, translator, broadcaster, drama critic and columnist, he has published five collections in English, a collection of poetry in Irish and translations from Catalan and Galaicoportuguese.

Leeds Nó Amsterdam
(do Liam Ó Brádaigh)

I do phóca, ag stánadh amach,
feadóg stáin. Ollóineach súgach
fiosrach amháin. Ansan go h-obann
chuir tú preab sa gceol
The Boys of Blue Hill agus Planxty Drury
cuireadh deire leis an juke-box
is bhí an teach go léir ag damhsa linn,
bhí lucht an óil seolta agat
fé lán-cheol agat:
níor bhlaiseadar riamh, ina dTír-fó-Thuinn,
a leithéid de ghrá.

Amsterdamhsa go deo, a chroí,
dit orgel heeft in Kapstad gespeelt.

Leeds or Amsterdam
(for Liam Ó Brádaigh)

Sticking out of your pocket,
a tin-whistle. Just one inquisitive
Dutchman. Then suddenly you
set the music jumping:
The Boys of the Blue Hill and Planxty Drury,
that put a stop to the juke-box,
the whole pub was dancing with us,
you'd launched the drinkers into
full sail of music:
they'd never in their Lowlands tasted
such love before.

Amsterdancing for ever, friend:
dit orgel heeft in Kapstad gespeelt.

Sa Regent i Leeds má bhí Sasanach uaigneach
amháin ann, b'in an méid. Ní raibh deoch ba throime
ná liomonáid bhuí ag Cathal ach bhí Planxty
Johnson go deo aige, bhí Liam Óg ann
agus Sligomen in town, agus bunadh cheoil nach iad
agus lucht óil nach iad, an ceol á shlogadh siar
    againn:
arsa mise le Francie i dteach an asail
'Here we are' agus thóg sé na focail as mo bhéal
'in the heart of England'—
'in the heart of Ireland' arsa mise dhá cheartú:

Dhá mhí-cheartú, mo léan géar—
súgradh searbh, Iain-lom—
'It looks as if,' arsa Vladimir Ilyitch, tráth,
'we'll have to go underground again.' Agus tá
an chuma sin air anois, a chroí:
ach nach muidne atá cleachtaithe
ar an gcleas úd, ar an gceol úd?
Seans nach mbeidh ceol na mbriathar fágtha againn
seans nach mbeidh fágtha againn go luath
ach feadóg stáin.

In the Regent in Leeds there was just one lonely
Englishman; bar us. Lemonade was the strongest
Cathal would take but he had Planxty
Johnson for ever, Liam Óg was there
and Sligomen in town, and others making
music besides them and others drinking
and all of us gulping down the music, I said
to Francie in the jax
'Here we are,' and he took the words out of my
      mouth
'in the heart of England'—
'in the heart of Ireland' said I correcting him:

Miscorrecting him: 'It looks
as if,' said Vladimir Ilyitch once
'we'll have to go underground again.'
And that's the way it looks now, dear heart:
but aren't we a people well trained
to that trick, to that music?
We may come to lose the music of our words,
we may lose everything soon—
except a tin-whistle or two.

Translated by the author

Is Trua Nach Loscáin Sinn

Thosaigh na loscáin ag breith
níos doimhne ná riamh, ag tabhairt
le tuiscint don fheirmeoir eolach
go raibh samhradh fada álainn
te tirim in ann dúinn.

Bhaineamar taitneamh as an samhradh
'bhí beagnach comh brothallach álainn
leis na gnáth-shamraíocha
ag Franco 'gus a phobal ionmhuin.

Ní eireoidh leis choíche
arsa sean-fhile liom, lá,
ár ngrian ansin thuas a bhaint dínn,
ná ár spéir ghorm a bhaint dínn,
ná ár samhradh a bhaint dínn:
sin é an t-aon rud amháin
nach féidir leis a bhaint dínn—
's é ag síneadh a láimhe
i dtreo na spéire.

Seo é an dara samhradh fada álainn
te tirim aisteach, anseo.
An mbeidh na samhraíocha seo 'gainne
i gcónaí mar sin as seo amach?
An loiscfear fiú na loscáin?

Is dóigh go bhfuil sean-chleachtadh
ag loscáin na Spáinne
bheith ag breith a gcuid uibheacha
go domhain domhain
    domhain

Baile Átha Cliath, Samhradh na hEagla: 1976

126

A Pity We're Not Frogs

The frogs began nesting
deeper than ever
so the wise farmer knew
we were in for a long beautiful
dry hot summer.

We enjoyed that summer, it was almost
as beautiful and almost as torrid
as the summers normally granted
Franco and his beloved people.

One thing he'll never be able for,
said an old poet to me one day,
is to take that sun up there away from us,
he can't take our weather away from us,
he can't take our summer—
that's the only thing
he can't take from us;
and the poet stretched his hand
up to the sky.

This is the second summer running here
that's long, beautiful, dry, hot, strange.
Will our summers be always
like this from now on?
Will even the frogs get burnt?

The frogs in Spain are doubtless well-
used to laying
their eggs deep
            deep

Dublin,
The Summer of Fear: 1976
Translated by the author

Amhrán Bréagach

Dúradh léi gur manach búdach í
i mbeatha eile dá cuid fadó;
's gur fhág fós gan críochnú
dealbh mhór shuaimhneach an bhúda.
Gheall an cailín go gcríochnódh
sí féin an dealbh naofa.

Dá mb'fhíor athbhreith
cá bhfios nach dtiocfadh ar an saol arís
ambasadóir ina rúnaí óg,
ina chailín? iarla ríoga
ina bhádóir óg, ina bhuachaill
cúig bliana déag d'aois
ar loch geal na síochána?
clúmh-agus-tarradóir ina bhean óg
i ngrá le saighdiúr gallda?
nó saighdiúr marfach aineolach
ina stailc ocrais,
ina bhró feamainne?

Nó gach duine mór-le-rá
ina dhuine?

Nó, ina fheithid—

Agus an bádóir óg
cá bhfios nach dtiocfadh ar ais
ina dhealbhadóir an áthais?

Lying Song

Long ago in a different life,
they told her, she had been
a Buddhist monk, but left unfinished
a big serene carving
of Buddha himself. The girl swore
she'd finish the holy sculpture
this time round.

Rebirth if true, who knows
but some ambassador might come back to life
as a young secretary, a girl?
a royal earl get re-born
a boatman; a boy
of only fifteen years
on some bright lake of peace?
a tar-and-feather merchant
as a young woman in love with a foreign soldier?
or a murderous ignorant soldier
as a hunger-strike
or a mass of floating seaweed?

Or every VIP
as just a human being?

Or, an insect—

Who knows but the young
boatman might come back
a sculptor of happiness?

Translated by the author

BIDDY JENKINSON

Biddy Jenkinson writes only in Irish. Her work has been published in *Innti*, *Poetry Ireland*, *Comhar*, *Feasta*, *Déirdre* and *Riverine*. Her first collection was *Baisteadh Gintlí* (1987), her second, *Uiscí Beatha*, was published in 1988.

Ciúnas

Fáilte romhat a bhradáin bhig
a chaith an bhroinn le confadh saoil.
Gabhaim orm bheith mar abhainn
dod chúrsa óm chom go sáile i gcéin.

Scaoil do racht is ól go faíoch.
Súigh uaim suan. I gconradh cíche
súfad siar ó lúb do bheoil
gean le tál arís go buíoch.

Fáilte romhat a bhradáin suain
dhein lánlinn chiúin i sruth mo shaoil.
Ar sheol do chuisle airím ceol
na nUile dom sheoladh féin.

Silence

How I welcome you, little salmon
who leapt the womb, impatient to commence life.
I undertake to be a river to you
as you follow your course from the haven of
      my belly to far distant seas.

Let yourself go, and drink up your fill.
Suck sleep from me. By the terms of the breast-
      contract
I'll suck back from your puckered lips
love, with which I'll suckle another time, and for that
      I'm grateful.

How I welcome you, salmon of sleep
who made a tranquil pool in my life-stream.
In the rhythm of your heartbeat
I hear the music of the Heavens,
      and it guides my way.

Translated by Pádraigín Riggs

MUIRIS Ó RÍORDÁIN

Muiris Ó Ríordáin was born in Abbeydorney, Co. Kerry in 1930. A lecturer in Mary Immaculate College of Education, Limerick, his poetry has been published in various magazines and journals, and has been anthologised in *Nuafhilí 2* (1968). He died in 1993.

Ar Fheiceáil Nóta I Leabhar Staire Dom

Is maith liom tú a bheith, a bhuachaill ar aimsir,
Faoi dheireadh id'nóta i leabhar ag lucht
    taighde,
Má scríobhann siad le peann faoi dhrochmheas
    is íde,
Le do chorpsa do scríobh tú faoi fhulaingt gan
    faoiseamh.

Chloisinn do churfá Domhnach is
    dálach:
'Tar agus cuir agus aistrigh is
    ardaigh,
Caith agus téir agus tabhair agus
    láimhsigh,
Crom agus rómhar agus cad tá ad'choimeádsa?'

On Seeing a Note in a History Text

Servant boy, I'm very happy that at last there is a note
In a very learned journal that made reference to your
      rôle.
If with pens they write of insults, of demeaning tasks
      prescribed,
With your body you have written of the sufferings
      and the times.

Every morning came your chorus, Sunday, Monday,
      every day,
'Come and put and shift and lift it, lift it higher in the
      air,
Come on now, catch and handle and don't let it get
      away,
Bend and dig and hurry, hurry, do you think we've
      got all day?'

Sa ghort duit lá seaca is an ghrian i do thimpeall,
Do chapaill ag tarraingt an chéachta go
    maorga,
Cé thiocfadh suas leat ach uaisleacht is
    aoibhneas
Le gradam is le cumas is le hársacht do cheirde.

D'fhillis tar éis treafa go láthair do
    náire,
D'imigh an uaisleacht 's an binneas ód'
    lámha,
Chuala tú gíoscadh an phaidirín chnáimh-
    seálaigh,
'Crom agus rómhar agus cad tá ad'
    choimeádsa?'

Is iomaí sin oíche is tú ag déanamh ar
    bhaile,
Is iomaí sin maidin is an geimhreadh ag
    spealadh,
Gur las ionat caor a mharódh le mire,
Ach mhaolaigh an fhearg i láthair an
    duine.

An ait leat, a stairí, gur mhúch sé a mhian,
Is gur ghaibh sé siúd tiarnas ar thearmann
    a chroí?
Ach ba chuimhin leis siúd maidin is na capaill
    ar srian,
Is an uaisleacht is an t-uaigneas a ghaibh é sa
    ghort,
Is gan ceannas ag éinne ar shaoirse na
    mbocht.

On a frosty, sun-filled morning in a field I saw you
      plough,
Horses straining at the traces, moving splendidly and
      proud,
When what should come beside but nobility and grace
In the dignity and beauty of your venerable trade.

When you had finished ploughing to the farmyard you
      came,
What was noble and was gracious from around you
      fell away,
You heard the tedious chorus, the predictable
      complaint,
'Bend and dig and hurry, hurry, do you think we've
      got all day!'

There was many a weary evening as you walked home,
There was many a winter morning that was searing,
      searing cold,
When a fury burst within you that was murderous like
      fire,
But your soul contained your fury in the presence of
      your mind.

You may find it strange, O scholar, that he could
      contain such fire,
That he should control the passion of his natural desire,
But he had known a morning with his horses in the
      field
When beside him walked nobility and loneliness and
      peace,
When the freedom of the poor man was no one's gift
      to give or keep.

                                    Translated by the author

Agus Mé Ocht mBliana Déag

Cailín le beartáin crochta ar gach méar aici,
Chonac ar shráideanna na cathrach aréir,
An cóta, an folt dubh is na beola a bhí daite,
Lasair 'na súile is an gáire ar a béal.

Is eol dom an gleann as a dtáinig an cailín,
Aithne agam uirthi ó bhí sí 'na naí,
Cuimhim liom cosnochta í, óg agus crosta í,
Páiste gealgháireach mo shean-pháirtí.

Níl sí sa chathair ach scaitheamh beag gairid,
Ach féach ar an athrú a tháinig gan mhoill,
Chuala sí ceolta is plódadh na slóite,
Is tháinig an fiabhras ar a dtugtar B'l'Áth' Cliath.

Rachaidh sí abhaile um Nollaig go spleodrach,
Cuirfidh éad ar na cailíní d'fhag sí 'na diaidh,
N'fheadar a' gcuimhneoidh sí ar an gcéad uair a
        phógas í,
Oíche na Nollag ag binn bhán an tí.

The Christmas I was Eighteen

A girl with parcels hung on her fingers,
Out in the city I noticed last night,
Her coat and her hair and her lipstick and laughter,
And her eyes were a flood of shining delight.

I know her name and the place that she came from,
The world of her childhood was my world too,
I remember the barefooted, mischievous tomboy,
And she laughed, I remember, the greyest day
      through.

I heard that she'd come to the city last summer.
Look at the changes the city has wrought:
She hears all its music, responds to its rhythms,
The fever exultant has gladly been caught.

She will go home resplendent this Christmas,
Trailing the envy her coming has brought.
I wonder if she will remember I kissed her
For the first time that Christmas by the white gable
      wall.

Translated by the author

SEÁN Ó hÉIGEARTAIGH

Seán Ó hÉigeartaigh was born in Cobh, Co. Cork in 1931. A teacher, schools' inspector and lecturer, his first collection, *Cama-Shiúlta*, appeared in 1964.

Marbhna Tar Éis Cóisire

Lá 'le Pádraig, Páras, 1958

Sheoladar aníos ar an oíche chugainn
go dtí an t-árasán thuas faoi na frathacha—
mionfhuaimeanna pearsanta na cathrach
a bhí á searradh féin roimh dhul a luí.
Bhí glór ag gluaisteáin thall is abhus
mar bheadh ag píosa cadáis dá stracadh
gan choinne sa seomra béal dorais.
Agus an corr-Arabach a bhí ag filleadh abhaile
méadaíodh ar mhacalla a choisíochta
gur dhein fathach de sa doircheacht thíos
a samhlófá miodóg leis go cúng ina chrios.

Bhí an slua iltíreach imithe abhaile
is seamaí cainte leo go binn ar a mbeola
faoin oileáinín aisteach iathghlas
ar shamhailt a mhuintir ar chinnteacht cine
pé áit sa domhan ina rabhadar ar fán.
Is ba chraitheadh as mealbhóg na cinniúna
a d'fhág ar aon láthair an ceathrar againn
ar bheag é ár gcaidreamh pearsanta
is ár n-aird ar raonta a chéile.

Post Festive Lament

St Patrick's Day, Paris, 1958

They drifted upwards on the night
upwards to the apartment beneath the rafters,
the little personal sounds of the city
which was stretching itself before sleep.
A car sounded here and there
as if a piece of cotton were being torn
unexpectedly in the room next door.
And the occasional Arabian returning home,
the echo of his footsteps was amplified
until he became a giant in the darkness below
of whom one imagined a slender knife in his belt.

The cosmopolitan crowd had gone home,
polished words on their eloquent lips
concerning that strange green-meadowed little island
whose people were an example of certainty of race
wherever on earth they wandered.
A shake of fate's pouch it was
had left on the one spot the four of us,
four of little personal acquaintance
or interest in one another's paths.

Smut de choinneal i scroig bhuidéal fíona,
is na ballaí ag liongáil le gach siolla gaoithe
a d'éalaigh trí bhéal na fuinneoige isteach.

Ina shuí leis fein i gcúinne den seomra
bhí an fealsamh féasógach ó Chluain Tarbh.
Ina charraig bháite a thaibhsigh sé riamh
i bhfarraige na seanchuimhní smuguaine,
is é ag feitheamh go hadhmaintiúil
leis an mborradh sin i dtaoide na Gaeilge
a chuirfeadh barc beag liteartha eile
ar snámh faoi dhéin a chuid méiscrí crua.
Ní nochtann riamh ann aon spleodar anama
ná aon taitneamh fíor i mbeatha na tíre
mura mbíonn longbhriseadh á bheartú aige,
nó mura bhfeiceann sé maidhm teichte eile
á chur ar 'na dúchasaigh nua seo'.

Sa bhreacarnach meathsholas is scáile
a dhlúthaigh an tsíleáil anuas ar na ballaí
bhí ceol ag osnaíl as an orgán béil.

Labhair an ceannaí ó Chaisleán Ó gConaing
is amhrán á lorg aige in onóir na tíre,
agus do scoilt soir siar ina dhá leath.
Bhí caint bhreá thíriúil Uí Cairbre Aobhdha
i ngleic le bogás ceannasach a shúl
is lena bhréidíní míne scothfhaisiúnta.
Chuaigh sé ag dornfhásc leis siar amach,
thar bhallaí fíonsmeartha an árasáin,
thar bhlianta seasca an mhéithris,
go dtí dúiche fhadshaolach na hóige.

The stub of the candle in the neck of a wine bottle,
the walls undulating with every syllable of wind
that stole in through the mouth of the window.

Sitting by himself in the corner of the room
was the bearded philosopher from Clontarf.
A submerged rock he had always seemed
in the sea of old snot-green memories,
as he awaited magnetically
that swelling in the tide of Irish
which would send another small literary barque
floating towards his cruel fissures.
He never shows any exuberance of spirit
or genuine pleasure in the life of the country,
unless he is planning a shipwreck,
or unless he sees these latest natives
in routed flight once again.

In the weak and mottled light and shadow
which pressed the ceiling down upon the walls
music sobbed from the mouth organ.

The dealer from Castle Connell spoke,
seeking a song in the country's honour,
and split east and west in two halves.
The fine country speech of Carberry of the Maigue
conflicted with the masterful complacency of his ey
and with the soft fashionable tweeds.
He hand fished back beyond the
wine smeared walls of the apartment,
beyond the fat infertile years
to the long lived place of his youth.

Ach dá dhéine a chuardach ar thóir a shealbha
níor bhuail leis de na seoda iomadúla
ach focail bheaga as rabhcán sráide.

An choinneal go guagach ag luascadh an tseomra,
is smaointe féin ar seachrán gan stró ar bith
faoi bhrat an tsuaimhnis ar an seachtú hurlár.

Ina splanc gheal den bhfuinneamh fuar
sea shamhlaíos riamh é, an file fionn seo
a shiúlaigh isteach sa ghluaiseacht lá.
Ar feadh cúpla mí chuaigh sé le craobhacha
na Gaeilge míne i nDuibhneachaibh ársa,
ionas go mbainfeadh sé clocha scáil
i gCoimíneoil na seorthaí líofa,
is go sábháilfí an barr beag scáinte.
Ach níorbh aon tslat draíochta aige
feac fhadharcánach na sluaiste,
ná aon ribín réidh go dtí Teamhair na Rí
an scabhat caol anacair go barr an
        aird.
Amach as an gcúngrach anama chúlaigh sé
chomh gasta le cat an bhainne scólta;
agus feasta d'fhógair le nimhneachas naofa
a bhfaca sé de bhaol is de dhiomailt aimsire
i ngluaiseacht na ngealt sin a bheartaigh laincis
a chur ar sprid neamhtheimhlithe na hÉireann.

Maoineachas codlatach lonnaithe sa seomra,
cling ag gloiní ag cnagadh ar a chéile
is ré órga nua á lua againn go mórtasach.

But however keen his search for his estate,
of so many jewels, he happened upon
but a few words of a street shanty.

The wavering candle sways the room
and my wandering thoughts stray without effort
while cloaked tranquillity on the seventh floor.

As bright as a flash of cold energy
I had always imagined him, this fair poet
who walked into the movement one day.
For a few months he went wild about
soft Irish in ancient Corca Dhuibhne,
collecting quartz stones
in Coimineoil of the fluent phrases
that the slight small crop might be saved.
But the long horny handle of the spade
was not his magic wand,
nor was the narrow difficult defile to the top of the
        height
a smooth road to the Tara of the Kings.
Out of that congestion of soul he retreated
as quickly as the milk-scalded cat,
and denounced from then on with poisonous sanctity
the danger and waste of time he observed
in that movement of madmen
who planned to put a spancel
on the stainless spirit of Ireland.

Sleepy sentimentality settles in the room,
glasses clink when striking upon one another
as we speak of a new golden age with pride.

Sheasas liom féin ag béal na fuinneoige,
tamall ar leithligh óm' chompánaigh
a raibh suantraí acu á chuachadh os íseal.
Thar dhíonta na cathrach ó thuaidh
amuigh ar imeall na hEorpa
bhí an tír a mhúnlaigh sinn uile:
í mar abhainn ann ag deireadh a cúrsa
a mbeadh a bruacha ag cur thar maoil
le huiscí gach srutha is gach séilteán
        sléibhe
a theagmhaigh riamh léi ina hiomramh.
Ba bhainc bheaga de raic leathbháite
mé féin is mo chomhathbheochantóirí,
seanfhrathacha as an Teach Míochuarta,
urlanna briste is meamraim smálaithe;
agus lenár n-ais bhí loingeas na tíre
ag scuabadh leo go snasta ar aghaidh
faoi dhéin tránna is cóstaí nua
ar a ngealfadh an maidneachan tuartha.
Ach nuair a bhogfaí sinn den scairbh
nó as tonn ar bogadh na riasc
le cóir ghaoithe nach gclisfeadh orainn,
ghluaisfimis ar a bhfuaid go maorga
is bheadh an cheannasaíocht chine go nua
ag teannadh cáblaí ár n-árthaigh
is ag bolgadh ár seolta go buach.

I stand alone at the mouth of the window,
a little aside from my companions,
who are quietly humming a lullaby.
Beyond the roofs of the city, northwards,
out on the edge of Europe
was the land which had moulded us all,
a river at the end of her course
whose banks were overflowing
with the waters of every stream and every mountain
     rivulet
which it had encountered in its course.
I and my co-revivalists were
small banks of half submerged wrack,
old rafters from Tara's Teach Miochuarta,
broken shafts, smudged memoranda,
while near us, the country's ships
were sweeping glossily onwards
to new strands and coasts
on which would brighten the augured morning.
But when we were eased off the reef
or off the quaking sod of the marsh
with a favourable wind which would not fail us
we would move among them imposingly
and leadership of the nation
would once again tense the cables of our vessels,
and swell our sails to victory.

Translated by Pádraig Mac Fhearghusa

ART Ó MAOLFABHAIL

Art Ó Maolfabhail was born in Limerick in 1932. He works
for the Placenames Commission. He has published two ac-
claimed collections of poetry.

Inis Córthaidh Agus Gné Den Stair

Is beag áit chomh hálainn dá bhfaca
le seandún Inis Córthaidh faoi ghealaigh
lán na Lúnasa go carthanach
ón ard anuas ag bánú peacaí
beaga suaracha nach fiú Dia a n-aire;
sea, is nach fiú daoine a ndéanamh.
Agus bánaítear peacaí na staire:
Ar Fhiodh na gCaor anseo ní shéantar
míle laoch i bhfuil gur thit, míle
laoch a deirtear leo, ach fir thréigthe
in andóchas beatha sea shílim
dóibh gur fearr do thuig bás méirligh
ná glóir a thuilleamh as bás le tírghrá.
Ar shráideanna sceamhacha an bhaile
anocht airím fir agus chím mná,
muintir chiúin bhéasach tirm gan aincis
ag trácht le ceart is le cruinnmhaíomh
ar cluichí gaile an náisiúin, insint
éachta Wexford, athinsint ar ghníomh
dhein Ned, Oliver, nó Jim English
ar son an chontae. As fuarlánchéill
nó as bogmheisce tig an díomas
in a nglór, nuair a fhaighid trácht ar
        'ninety-eight,

146

Enniscorthy and An Aspect of History

Few places have I seen
as lovely as Enniscorthy under a full
August moon lovingly
whitening from on high
small, insignificant sins not worth God's heed;
indeed, not even worth committing.
And the sins of history are forgiven:
On Vinegar Hill here no-one denies
the thousand men who fell,
a thousand heroes so regarded, but as men
abandoned to despair, I think of them,
who better understood a rebel's death
than to die in patriot's glory.
On the town's bleak streets tonight
I hear men, I see women,
A quiet, well-mannered, tranquil people
discussing and shrewdly praising
the valiant games of the nation, telling
of the exploits of Wexford, recounting the deeds
of Ned, Oliver or Jim English
for the County. In sober senses
or slightly tipsy the pride rises
in their voices when they tell of
         'ninety-eight,

ar phíce is ar an nglún bhí líonmhar,
an tseisiú glún sin uainn siar. Doirse
an leathadh agus ceol mear chun rince
mar is ionmhain ón radio ag doirteadh
in a thionlacain don ré ar dhúlinnte
guairneacha na Sláinne. I stuacanna
cheana tá an chruithneacht seasta ar garda
mar a sinsir d'fhas as corp an bhuachalla
chlaíte. Ach ní mór peacaí ró-ghránna
na staire a mhaitheamh agus téim síos
don teach aíochta. Síním m'ainm dílis
ar an duilleog don chailín geanúil. Fíor
don té chuir dea-chlú ar shaormhíne,
ar ghlanchinseal is ar thíorthúlacht
na ndaoine seo. Agus an stair má chlisfidh
cé mise ná maithfinn gan mí-rúnta
don ainnir adeir 'What's that in English?'

of pikes, and of the numerous people
of six generations ago. Doors
open and the usual lively dance-music
spilled from radios accompanies the moon
shining on the swirling black pools of the Slaney.
Already the wheat in stooks stands on guard
like their ancestors, who sprung from the bodies
of the slain croppies. But we must pardon
history's ugly sins and I go down
to the guest house. I sign my surname
in the book of the gentle girl. Well for him
who praised the gentleness,
the nobility and the homeliness
of these people. Even if history flinch:
Who am I that I wouldn't freely pardon
the girl who asked 'What's that in English?'

Translated by Gabriel Fitzmaurice

CONLETH ELLIS

Conleth Ellis was born in Carlow in 1937. A teacher, poet and critic, he has published nine collections of poetry in both Irish and English. He has won many prizes for his poetry and was awarded an Arts Council Bursary in 1982. He died in 1988.

Bua

Scéal a chuala mé nuair a bhí mé óg
Mar gheall ar Hogan clúiteach, an dealbhóir:

Nuair a nochtadh a shárobair san ardeaglais
S'gainne—íomhá de J K L, an t-easpag—

Tháinig mearbhall cinn air nuair a chonaic Hogan
Gur dhearmad sé fáinne 'chur ar an méar
        easpagóideach.

Chuaigh sé abhaile is chroch sé é féin
De bharr náire is déistin, deir an scéal.

Bhíos in amhras faoi fhírinne an scéil sin
Nuair a míníodh dom brí an 'Hogan fecit.'

Anois nuair a chaithim uaim dán eile marbh-bheirth
Chím Hogan ag cuimilt a dheilbhe gan teimheal.

Triumph

When I was young I heard this story
About the famous artist, Hogan:

How when they unveiled in our cathedral
His masterly sculpture of Bishop J K L.

Hogan as good as flipped his lid
Seeing he'd forgotten the episcopal ring.

He slipped off home and hanged himself
Through shame and disgust, the story said.

I doubted the truth of all such yarns
As soon as I learned what 'Hogan fecit' means.

Now when I discard another stillborn verse
I can see Hogan give his flawless statue a caress.

Translated by the author

As *Seabhac Ag Guairdeall (Gan Teideal)*

Cáil uirthi, m'aintín Cáit
As a teacht slán ón *Titanic*
    Chuaigh buille na tubaiste
    Amú an oíche sin.

An t-aon uair a chonaic mise í
Ba ar éigean a bhí sí beo.
    Ar éigean a bhrúigh séala a hanama
    Anuas ar chéir a leapa.

'Seo,' arsa m'uncail Jack,
'Gasúr Bhríde, an dara mac.'
    Ba leasc liom druidim isteach
    Faoi chnoc oighir na hailse.

Síneadh lámh i mo threo,
Cnámha i gclúdach litreach.
    'Tabhair braon líomanáide dó, Jack.'
    Bhí tiúilipí i mbláthchuach.

Bhíos an-bheag, an-ghar dá haghaidh,
Greim láimhe ag na mairbh orm.
    Ar aigéan bán, ar aigéan ciúin
    Bhíos i mbaol mo bháite.

Untitled from *Seabhac ag Guairdeall* (*A Hawk Circling*)

Famous, my auntie Kate
For surviving the *Titanic*.
    The *coup de grace* strayed
    Off target that night.

The one time I saw her
She was scarcely alive,
    Her soul's seal barely pressing
    Into the wax that was her bed.

'This,' said my uncle Jack,
'Is Bridie's young fellow, the second.'
    I was loth to sail in
    Under the iceberg of cancer.

A hand stretched towards me,
An envelope of bones.
    'Give him a drop of lemonade, Jack.'
    There were tulips in a vase.

I was very small, very near her face.
The dead had me by the hand.
    On a white ocean, on a calm ocean
    I was in danger of drowning.

Translated by the author

As *Seabhac ag Guairdeall* *(GanTeideal)*

Muid thíos, is dócha, ag bun na sráide
Ar ár n-oileán diamhair, na Gilidíní,
Mo mháthair ag cniotáil, ag rá
Seachnaígí an poll srutha.

Bád canála ag siosamar thart,
Ár long fheileastraim líonta ag an tonn.
Próca suibhe againn lán go béal,
Gilidíní ar guairdeall ann.

Lúnasa '45, lán na sráide againn
I bhfostú i ngréasán an tsamhraidh.
Gilidíní sa dabhach folctha sa bhaile,
Muid dulta i dtaithí ar bhoige a mbáis.

An lá a séideadh Hiroshima chun siúil
Muid ag lapadaíl, is dócha, san abhainn,
Gilidíní ina gcith ar an uisce,
Ina ngealscamall faoin chraiceann.

An lá a ghealaigh an fhrithghrian
As ar fhás scamall na ciontachta
Gilidíní á gceapadh, is dócha, againn
In eangach phollta an deireanais.

Untitled from *Seabhac ag Guairdeall* (*A Hawk Circling*)

I suppose we were at the bottom of the street
On our secret island, the Minnow,
My mother knitting and calling out
Keep away from the hole when you paddle.

A canal boat rustling past,
Our flag boat drowned in its wash,
A jam-jar full to the rim
With minnows going round and round.

A whole streetful of us in August '45
Caught in the webs of the summer.
The soft deaths of the minnow at home
In the bathtub no longer a shock.

The day Hiroshima was blown sky high
I suppose we were knee-deep again,
Minnow like a shower on the water,
Like a bright cloud under its skin.

The day the anti-sun dawned
Giving birth to the gloom of our guilt
I suppose we were catching minnow
In a torn net late into the night.

Translated by the author

As *Seabhac ag Guairdeall* (Gan Teideal)

An táilliúir a tháinig leis an lá
Ar an gcorp, é ag siúl
De réir a ghnáis an chosáin
Tarraingthe i dtreo an droichid.

An rópa a thug sé ar dtús faoi deara,
É ceangailte den bhalla eibhir
Áit a thagadh na báid canála
Le cé, teannadh ar an ngad.

Fear tuisceanach smaointeach,
A rothar ina leaslúí lena ais,
Níor theastaigh uaidh, dúradh,
Go scuabfaí le sruth a fhadhb.

An abhainn á cur ag an tuile
Beagnach thar bruach, ní ligtear dúinn,
Cosmhuintir shráid an fhir bháite
Shráid an táilliúra, dul ina ghar.

Ach, an saol arís faoi smacht
Laethe fada an ghrianchloig, beimid
Ag princeam arís ansin, ag snámh,
Eala bhalbh ag oiliúint áil taobh linn.

Untitled from *Seabhac ag Guairdeall* (*A Hawk Circling*)

It was the tailor came
On the body at break of day
As he walked the towpath, as every
Working morning, towards the bridge.

The rope caught his attention first
Looped through the granite wall
Where the canal boats once tied up
The noose strained with the weight.

A sensible, thoughtful man,
His bicycle aslant nearby,
He had not wished, they said, the crux
He reached to be swept downstream.

The riverbank almost awash,
We from the drowned man's street,
From the street of the tailor,
Are not allowed near to the flood.

But long sunburnt days, order
Restored to the world, we will play
Here and swim while a mute swan
Raises her brood right beside us.

Translated by the author

TOMÁS MAC SÍOMÓIN

Tomás Mac Síomóin was born in Dublin in 1938. A poet and short story writer, his first collection, *Damhna agus Dánta Eile* (1974), won an Arts Council Award in 1977.

Treoir

Léim isteach in aol an fhocail
is spáinfear duit críocha

léim isteach in eibhear mo bhéarsa
is spáinfear duit púicín
na gréine ciartha

léim isteach i bpóca mo chnis
do shúil ní dhallfar
ar shúil na gaoithe

caith a goirme-siúd isteach
i ndianbhruith láibe
brúigh go domhain isteach é
le rinn do shála

fág trí lá é
fág trí oíche
go bhfásfaidh an focal
as gorm na gaoithe

Direction

Climb onto the limestone of the word
and lands shall be shown unto you

climb into the granite of my verse
and you shall be shown the blindfold
of a sun made dark

climb into the pocket of my skin
and your eye shall come to recognise
the eye of the wind

cast its blue
into mud on the boil
thrust it in deeply
with the point of your heel

leave it three days
leave it three nights
until the new word grows
from the blue of the wind

focal broinne
focal brácha

imigh leat a chleite
le gaoth an fhocail úd

womb-word
judgement-day-word
clean as snow
outpacing the wind

begone quickly, feather
on the wings of its slipstream

Translated by the author

Focal

Shníomhadar le díocas
Snáth na tola
Shealbhaigh carraig
Is cuan maguaird
Chraith síol rábach
Ar loime an bhranair
D'ardaigh sconnsaí
Bhain an barr is
Shníomh le dua
Snáth a n-allais
Nuair shín an bhaineannach
Fúthu sa leapa
Shníomh le teaspach
Snáth na fola
Líon na tithe
Thóg iasc go barra
Thomhais a gceol
Le dord na mara
Gur chas faoi dheoidh
Súgán a bhfocail;
Ach tréigeadh cuan
Is tréigeadh carraig
Cré na cille
Ramhraigh, rathaigh
Is chonaic fiach dubh

Word

Eagerly they spun
The thread of will
Seized the rock
And surrounding seas
Cast generous seed
On fallow earth
Raised their walls
Took in their crops
Spun in hardship
The thread of sweat
Lay with their women
In the bed
Spun with ardour
The thread of blood
Filled the houses
Caught the fish
Matched their song
To ocean drone
Braided at last
The rope of their word.
Sea was abandoned
Then the rock
Clay of the graveyard
Grew rich and fat
I saw the raven

Ar charraig thréigthe
Snáth na tola
I ngob na bréine
Snáth na fola
I mbéal mná rialta
Is snáth an allais
Ag slogaire otraithe
De statsheirbhíseach
Adúirt: 'N'fheadar conas
A litreofaí san
De réir an chaighdeáin?'

On that rock
Thread of will
In a loathsome beak
Thread of blood
In the mouth of a nun
And the thread of sweat
In the beery mouth
Of a bloated civil servant
Who said: I wonder how
We'd spell that now
According to the Official Standard?

Translated by the author

Aogán

'Amhráin ar an sean-nós—
Ní fiú sop tuí iad!'
Do mháigh urlabhraí de chlann
An bhrise,
'Is tá ré na sua
Le bheith feasta ar lár;
Ar dhán do chroí
Níl rachairt nó éileamh;
Tréig, a fhile, fuaruabhar do cheirde!
Fógair fán ar chlann, ar chnis!

'Samhail a bheirim inniu dod' ghin:
Uaigh ar an aineol
Ag an bhfile a réabadh
Gan leac nó lodairne os a cionn
D'fhógródh tásc na gcnámh d'éinneach.'

'Nuair a shiúlaim abuil mo dháin
Ar neamhcheist le gramaisc a' Bhéarla
Chímse Mór na Múmhan
Go teann im' dháil ag téarnamh,
Is mairfidh mo dhán go buan
Ar bhinnbhéal úd na sméar,
Is golfairt agus gáire na sua,'
Aduirt an Rathailleach, Éigeas.

Aogán

'Your sean-nós song
Isn't worth a straw!'
Said a spokesman of the
Defeated tribe,
'Heroes live
In history books;
The public taste
Rejects your song;
Abandon, poet, your craft's cold pride,
Loom, weft and warping frame.

'The image I give your art today
Is an unknown grave
That a poet digs;
No stone above proclaims
The tale of the bone that lies there.'

'When I walk beside my darling,
Heedless of the rabble of the English tongue,
I see great Mór of Munster
With hurried step approach.
My song will live forever
On Mór's sweet berry-red lips
And the weeping and laughter of heroes,'
Said Aogan Ó Rathaille, Poet.

Translated by the author

167

Celan

Stroic crag airgid croí Celan
Glan eascartha amach as cis a chráimh
Is thit a dhaingean síos isteach
I mbóchna bhaoth an bháis.
Ach mhair an briathar a chan sé an oíche úd.
Ag bóithreoireacht feadh na mblianta
Gur shaigh an eochair i mbeo mo chré
A d'oscail athuair an chréacht úd.
Is féach, a Celan, fuil chraorag do chroí
A' sileadh thar chab mo dháin
Is an síol a chuiris fadó riamh
Ag scoilteadh leac an bháis.

Celan

A silver claw tore Celan's heart
Clean out of its cage of bone
And down his ramparts tumbled
Into Death's idiot ocean.
But the word he sang that night lived
On and roamed the roads of time,
Placed a key in this living clay
That opened again that wound.
And, Celan, see your heart's red blood
Spurt across this lip of Gaelic verse;
See the seed you planted then
Split the mould of death.

Translated by the author

MÍCHEÁL Ó hAIRTNÉIDE

Mícheál Ó hAirtnéide (Michael Hartnett) was born in Croom, Co. Limerick in 1941. He spent his youth in Newcastle West, Co. Limerick. His first collection, *Anatomy of a Cliché* (1968) was rightly acclaimed. Established as a major voice in contemporary Irish poetry in the English language, he returned to West Limerick in 1975 and for the next ten years devoted himself to writing in Irish only. Now living in Dublin, he writes both in Irish and English.

As *An Phurgóid*

Faic filíochta níor scríobh mé le fada
gé go dtagann na línte mar théada damháin alla—
prislíní Samhna ag foluain trí gharrán:
an scuaine meafar ag tuirling orm,
na seanshiombailí—'an spéir atá gorm,
póg agus fuiseog agus tuar ceatha'—
ábhar dáin, a bhás is a bheatha.

Anois ó táim im thiarna talún
ar orlach inchinne, ní dheinim botún
ach cuirim as seilbh na samhla leamha—
na hinseacha meirgeacha, na rachtanna lofa,
cabáil is tagairt is iad go tiubh mar screamha
ar an aigne bán, ar an anam folamh.

From *The Purge*

Hartnett, the poet, might as well be dead,
enmeshed in symbol—the fly in the web;
and November dribbles through the groves
and metaphors descend on him in droves:
the blood-sucked symbols—the sky so blue,
the lark, the kiss, and the rainbow too.
This syrupy drivel would make you puke.

The monarch now of an inch of vision,
I'll not fall down for indecision
but banish for now and forever after
the rusty hinges, the rotten rafters,
the symbols, the cant, the high allusion
that reduce the white mind to confusion.

Sea, tagann an tinfeadh, ach níl mé sásta—
Clagairt poigheachán seilide atá fágtha
is carn crotail ciaróg marbh é,
an dán millte le baothráiteas
tá ag sú na fola as ealaín ársa
mar sciortán ar mhagairle madra.

Caithfidh mé mo chaint a ghlanadh is a fheannadh
nó gan phurgóid tuitfidh trompheannaid—
ní bheidh i ndán ach gaoth is glicbhéarla
is caillfidh mé mo theanga daonna . . .

. . . Éist aríst leis—clagairt cloiginn mo shean-
      mháthar
ar an staighre: cliotaráil easna m'uncail
im phóca (an siansa cnámh so)—
béic an tSagairt is scréach an Bhráthar—
an t-anam goilliúnach i súilibh m'athar:
laethanta m'óige (an cogar glórghránna).
Mórshiúl dorcha mo ghaolta am leanúint,
Uncail Urghráin agus Aintín Ainnis:
adhraim iad go léir is a seanchuilteanna
mar bíonn ar fhile bheith dílís dá fhoinse.
Caitheann sé muince fiacal a mháthar
is ceanglann sé leabhair le craiceann a dhearthár—
cruthantóir seithí, adhlacóir is súdaire.
Is peannaid shíoraí an oscailt uaigh seo—
bíonn na filí sa reilg gach uair a' chloig
ag troid ar son cnámh le ramhainn is sluasaid—
duine is snas á chur ar phlaitín a dhearféar aige
duine len bhroinn a rug é a' scríobadh cruimh aisti.
Gach dán ina liodán, marbhna nó caoineadh
is boladh na nglún fuafar ag teacht ó gach líne
is timpeall muiníl gach file, lán d'iarsmaí seirge,

172

Inspiration comes, and the poet is left
with the empty rattle of discarded shells,
the husks of beetles piled up dead—
his poem spoiled by stupid talk
that sucks the blood of an ancient craft
like a bloated tick on a mongrel's balls.

I must purge my thought and flay my diction
or else suffer that fierce affliction—
my poems only wind and bombast
having lost their human language . . .

. . . My uncle's ribs are clattering
in my pocket. And hear again—
on the stairs the cacophony
of granny's skull (this symphony
of bones)—Priest's and Brother's cries—
the wounded soul in my father's eyes:
the coarse whisper of my youth.
My ancestors march in dark pursuit:
Uncle Hate and Auntie Guilt,
I adore you both and your ancient quilts:
a poet must be true to his sources.
He wears a necklace of his mother's teeth;
with his brother's skin, his book's bound neat;
he's a curer of skins, a burier of corpses.
An eternal penance, this opening of graves—
the poets in the graveyards always with spades
and shovels fighting over bones—
one shines his sister's kneecap's dome,
one scrapes maggots from his mother's womb.
Each poem an elegy, a litany, or lament;
each line morbid with the hideous dead;
and hung around each poet's neck

tá taise a athar, a chadairne chóirithe . . .

. . . Ní file go máistir focal, ní file go ceard
ní file go hoiliúnt, ní file go fios dán—
gach dán atá ar domhan, a dhéanamh is
    a cheolsan,
ach seachain na bratacha is clog lobhair an eolais,
seachain bheith id shaoithín is id leabhar beo:
ní file go fios datha, fios deilbhe is ceoil.
Ach ní thig leat dath a scríobh, ná siolla eibhir
a bhreacadh síos—sin gníomh file daibhir.
File a phléann fiúg, cuireann sé gaoth le gaoith
is deineann praiseach is prácas as obair na saoithe
ach nuair is bán sinn is folamh de ló nó istoíche
alpaimid leigheas na foghlama siar chun faoisimh
is tuislímid go sonasach go dtí an carn crotal
ag carbhas go socair i dtábhairne an tsotail—
ach ní beacha sinn tá lán t'réis taisteal círe
ach puchaí atá breoite t'réis foracan géarfhíona . . .

. . . Mise uaigh an dóchais is reilg na fírinne,
diúgaire cáile is alpaire fuílligh.
Ní dheisfidh córas na n-ard braonanuas mo chroíse
ná an poll im anam mar a shileann ann
    maoithneachas.
Athchruthaím mé féin le cluasa Plato,
le sróin Freud, le hórdóig Hegel,
fiacla Bergson is croiméal Nietzsche:
na baill a thugann don leathchorp íce.
Tá Buddha plódaithe isteach sa slua ionam,
tá teagasc críonna sean-Lao Tzu ionam:
tinneas goile im anam atá am chrá
is pléasctar mo chorp ina fhearthainn bhláth.

are the tanned relics of his father's scrotum . . .

. . . A poet must master words, must learn his trade;
must be schooled in poetry, know how poems are
    made;
every poem in the world, its song and make.
Avoid labels and lepers' bells,
avoid the pedant pedagogical:
no poet is without colour, without stone, without
    chord.
But colour and granite won't yield to words,
the impoverished poet's syllables.
The poet's fugues add wind to wind
and wreck the work of greater men,
but white and empty, day and night,
we dose ourselves with others' thought
and stumble blithely to the heap of husks
and carouse safely in the pub—
we're no bees replete in the hive
but drunken wasps in the height of horrors
from sucking too much vinegar . . .

. . . I am the grave of hope and the tomb of truth,
swiller of fame, gulper of residues.
The systems of great men will never mend
my heart's drop-down, the leak of sentiment.
I construct myself with Plato's ears,
Hegel's thumb, Freud's beard,
Nietzsche's 'tache and Bergson's teeth
to make my body whole, complete.
I add Buddha to the crush
and Lao Tzu's teachings are a must:
but a pain in my belly upsets my powers
and my body explodes in a rain of flowers,

Tuitim síos le mórchioth file—
agus bláthanna gan chumhra iad uile—
le ceannbháin Kant is aiteal Aristotle,
sáiste Schopenhauer: na fealsaimh is a sotal.
I measc na ngas is na ngéag ina gcoillte
bím mar leanbh ar strae i bpáirc iománaíochta:
cloisim an gháir mholta ón slua ann
ach ní fheicim ach na mílte cóta móra.

Mise Frankenstein agus a chréatúr
de bhaill is fuílleach is seile déanta . . .

. . . Níl sa ráiteas ach dán gan bhod—
ceiliúr nó sluaghairm—sin a chualamar.
Iomann don oifigeach mhustrach í—
fadó, ba Róisín Dubh ár dtír,
inniu ina taoiseach nó ina easóg le púicín
nó trá gainmheach le héan lán d'íle.
Sluaghairm tá uaithi anois is ní hiad dánta
ná amhráin ach an oiread, ach baothráiteas.
Is ceart don fhile bheith tréatúrach ina dhántaibh
ach bheith ina laoch is gunna ina láimh aige.
Ní fiú broim an dán sa charcar,
ní dhingfidh sé clogad, ní stopfaidh sé urchar:
ní chothóidh sé éinne in am tortha lofa,
ní bia sa chorcán é don chlann sa ghorta.
Go raibh gorta is cogadh ar na staraithe go deo,
go raibh na dánta tírghrácha ag an bpopstar ghlórac
Níl tír ag file ach amháin an Ceart,
níl muintir aige ach ualach taibhreamh.
Is féidir leis mealladh is muscailt is cáineadh

and down I come with a shower of poets—
oh, they're some flowers, these perfumed oafs
with juniper of Aristotle, bogcotton of Kant,
sage of Schopenhauer, arrogant.
Here in a wood among stem and branch
like a child lost at a hurling match,
I hear the cheering of lusty throats
and see only the hems of coats.

Oh, I am Frankenstein and his creature
made of spittle, and bits and pieces . . .

. . . Statement is castrated verse—
a cry, a slogan—so we've heard:
the hymn of the pompous clerk.
Once our country was Róisín Dubh:
today it's a warlord, a stoat with a hood,
a sandy beach with an oil-soaked bird.
Of slogans now you can take your pick—
not poems or songs but rhetoric.
Where verse is treacherous, 'tis fitting and right
for the poet to turn fighter with an armalite.
A poem in prison isn't worth a fart—
won't dent a helmet, won't stop a shot:
won't feed a soul when the harvest rots,
won't put food in hungry pots.
Famine and war to all historians!
May popstars roar our ballads glorious!
Justice is the poet's land:
he has no family but a load
of dreams to sting, and coax and goad

le focail nach fiú cannaí stáin leis.
Go léime buataisí ar an gcloigeann
a dhéanann dearmad ar chontúirt na hintuigse . . .

. . . Do chuaigh critic amú i ndán uair amháin:
ní fhaca sé aon suaitheantas ann.
Do bhrúigh sé gach míne ann faoi chos—
chuala mionbhrioscarnach: thosnaigh sé ag gol.
Thosnaigh sé ar a dhia a ghuí,
d'iarr sé cabhair ón ollscoil is a taibhsí.
'Díreach ar aghaidh' do fhreagair,' 'go líne fiche nao
is do bhí a chomhartha ann, tagairt do Dante:
d'aimsigh sé a shlí amach is an dán do mhol sé.
Ní fhaca sé an ceard ná na snas bhí ann
ná na rudaí rúnda míne bhí lán de chumhacht—
ach amháin an suaitheantas gan slacht.
Bhí a chompás gan tairbhe insan áit
Nach raibh aon tuaisceart ann le fáil.
Cad is critic ann, in ainm Bhríde bheo?
Nó an bhfuil aon 'chomhchoibhneas oibiachtúil'
       ann dó?'

Cad tá fágtha nuair a chríochnaíonn an píobaire?
Dríodar, seile, macalla is triacla.

Bheul, tar éis sin uilig, tá an fhadhb fós fághta:
an dán a mhairfidh, an mbeidh sé daonna?
Brisim mo riail féin mar ní riail é
ach uím bheithigh de leathar déanta,
ceangailte ormsa, miúl na héigse.

Gé seift mise, táim aonarach.
Táim umhal is táim sotalach,
is inbhriste iad mo rialacha:

with words as worthless as tin cans.
May heavy boots stomp on the head
that forgets the danger of being understood . . .

. . . A critic floundered in a poem once
for want of signposts, the poor dunce.
He crushed each subtlety underfoot
and wept, hearing their brittle crunch.
He prayed to God that he might see,
he invoked the ghosts of the University.
'Straight ahead,' came the blessed answer,
'to line twenty-nine, and look for Dante,'
and released, he praised the poem, the chancer.
He saw no polish, or craft, or care,
nor the subtle power of the poet aware—
only that ugly signpost there.
His compass was of no account
in a place that had no north or south.
What's a critic, in the name of Bridget,
or can any 'objective correlative' gauge it?

So, what is left when the piper ceases?
Dregs, spit, echoes, and treacle.

There's still a problem, all said and done:
the poem that lives, will it be human?
I break my dictum—it's not a rule
but a harness on me, poetry's mule.

I am a conspiracy of one.
I'm humble, arrogant; when all is done
my rules are easily broken:

líon deich leabhar chun rá: ná habair faic.
Bí umhal don éiclips ach coimeád giota ré leat:
bí id sholas beag, bí id eisceacht.
Súigh an pluma is caith amach an eithne—
titfidh sí san aoileach
is beidh míle crann ag feitheamh leat.
Ná bí iomaíoch: níl againn ach dánta,
rudaí nach mbíonn rafar
faoi thaoiseach ná pápa.

Is seo í Éire, is mise mise.
Craobhscaoilim soiscéal an neamhaontaigh.
Obair ghrá is ealaíne, sin an méid a éilím
chomh folamh le nead gabha uisce
chomh bán le bolg gé.
Bóthar an fhile gan chlochmhíle air,
bóthar gan stad i n-óstan an ghrinn air,
bóthar le luibheanna gan aird air
ag bogadh go ciúin ó na claíocha áilne.

I fill ten books to say: let nothing spoken.
Serve the eclipse, keep a slice of the moon,
be a small light, be an exception too.
Suck the plumb, spit out the stone—
it will land on dung
and a thousand trees will grow.
Don't be competitive: all we have is poems,
things not answerable to leader or pope.

This is Ireland, and I'm myself,
I preach the gospel of non-assent.
Love and art is the work I want
as empty as a dipper's nest,
whiter than a goose's breast—
the poet's road with no milestone on it,
a road with no wayside stop upon it,
a road of insignificant herbs
welling quietly from every hedge.

Translated by Gabriel Fitzmaurice

Dán Do Rosemary

As an saol lofa seo
gabhaim leat leithscéal:
as an easpa airgid atá
ár síorsheilg thar pháirc
ár bpósta mar Fhionn
gan trua gan chion
ag bagairt ar do shacs-chroí bog ceanúil.
Gabhaim leat leithscéal
as an teach cloch-chlaonta
as fallaí de chré is de dheora déanta—
do dheora boga:
an clog leat ag cogarnach
ag insint bréag,
an teallach ag titim as a chéile.
Téim chugat ar mo leithscéal féin:
m'anam tuathalach, m'aigne i gcéin,
an aois i ngar dom, le dán i ngleic,
i mo gheocach sa tábhairne ag ól is ag reic.
Thréig mé an Béarla
ach leatsa níor thug mé cúl:
caithfidh mé mo cheird
a ghearradh as coill úr:
mar tá mo gharrán Béarla
crann-nochta seasc:
ach tá súil agam go bhfuil
lá do shonais ag teacht.
Cuirfidh mé síoda do mhianta ort lá
Aimseoimid beirt ár Meiriceá.

Poem for Rosemary

For this rotten world
I apologise to you:
for the lack of money
that's ever hunting the field
of our marriage like Fionn
without pity without love
threatening your gentle saxon heart.
I apologise to you
for this sloping homestead
for walls of earth and grieving made—
your soft tears:
the clock whispering
telling lies,
the hearth falling asunder.
I come to you with my alibis:
my awkward soul, my dreaming mind,
while age beckons, with poems I'm fighting,
a mummer in the pub, drinking, reciting.
I abandoned English
but never you:
I have to hone my craft
in a wood that's new:
for my English grove
is naked, barren:
but I hope your day
of happiness is coming.
You'll have the silk of your heart one day
we'll find us both our America.

Translated by Gabriel Fitzmaurice

CAITLÍN MAUDE

Caitlín Maude was born in Connemara, Co. Galway in 1941.
She was a poet, teacher, actress and traditional singer. She
wrote one play, *An Lasair Choille* (1961), with Michael Hart-
nett. Her poetry was published in various magazines and
journals. She died in Dublin in 1982. A collection, *Dánta*
(1984), was published posthumously. A prose play and two
later poems were published in *Caitlín* (1988).

Aimhréidh

Siúil, a ghrá,
cois trá anocht—
siúil agus cuir uait
na deora —
éirigh agus siúil anocht

    ná feac do ghlúin feasta
    ag uaigh sin an tsléibhe
tá na blátha sin feoite
agus tá mo chnámhasa dreoite . . .

    (Labhraim leat anocht
    ó íochtar mara—
    labhraim leat gach oíche
    ó íochtar mara . . .)

Entanglement

Walk, my love,
by the strand tonight—
walk, and away
with tears—
arise and walk tonight

    henceforth never bend your knee
    at that mountain grave
those flowers have withered
and my bones decayed ...

      (I speak to you tonight
      from the bottom of the sea—
      I speak to you each night
      from the bottom of the sea ...) ·

shiúileas lá cois trá—
shiúileas go híochtar trá—
rinne tonn súgradh le tonn—
ligh an cúr bán mo chosa—
d'árdaíos mo shúil go mall
'gus ansiúd amuigh ar an domhain
in aimhréidh cúir agus toinne
chonaic an t-uaigneas i do shúil
'gus an doilíos i do ghnúis

shiúileas amach ar an domhain
ó ghlúin go com
agus ó chom go guaille
nó gur slogadh mé
sa doilíos 'gus san uaigneas

once I walked on the strand—
I walked to the tide's edge—
wave played with wave—
the white foam licked my feet—
I slowly raised my eye
and there far out on the deep
in the tangle of foam and wave
I saw the loneliness in your eye
the sorrow in your face

I walked out on the deep
from knee to waist
and from waist to shoulder
until I was swallowed
in sorrow and loneliness

Translated by Gabriel Fitzmaurice

Amhrán Grá Vietnam

Dúirt siad go raibh muid gan náir
ag ceiliúr ár ngrá
agus an scrios seo inár dtimpeall

an seabhac ag guairdeall san aer
ag feitheamh le boladh an bháis

dúirt siad gurbh iad seo ár muintir féin
gurbh í seo sochraide ár muintire
gur chóir dúinn bheith sollúnta féin
bíodh nach raibh brónach

ach muidne
tá muid 'nós na haimsire
      go háirid an ghrian
ní thugann muid mórán aird'
ar imeachtaí na háite seo feasta

lobhann gach rud le teas na gréine
thar an mbás

agus ní muidne a mharaigh iad
ach sibhse

d'fhéadfadh muid fanacht ar pháirc an áir
ach chuir aighthe brónacha na saighdiúirí
ag gáirí sinn
agus thogh muid áit bhog cois abhann

Vietnam Love Song

They said that we were shameless
celebrating our love
with devastation all around us

the hawk hovering in the air
awaiting the stench of death

they said that these were our own
that this was the funeral of our own people
that we should at least be solemn
even if we were not mourning

but we
we are like the weather
    especially the sun
we don't pay much attention
to these happenings any longer

everything decays in the heat of the sun
after death

and it wasn't we who killed them
but you

we could have stayed on the field of slaughter
but the sad faces of the soldiers
made us laugh
and we chose a soft place by the river

Translated by Gabriel Fitzmaurice

Géibheann

Ainmhí mé

ainmhí allta
as na teochreasa
a bhfuil cliú agus cáil
ar mo scéimh

chroithfinn crainnte na coille
tráth
le mo gháir

ach anois
luím síos
agus breathnaím trí leathsúil
ar an gcrann aonraic sin thall

tagann na céadta daoine
chuile lá

a dhéanfadh rud ar bith
dom
ach mé a ligean amach

Captivity

I am an animal

a wild animal
from the tropics
  famous
  for my beauty

I would shake the trees of the forest
once
with my cry

but now
I lie down
and observe with one eye
the lone tree yonder

people come in hundreds
every day
who would do anything
for me
but set me free

Translated by Gabriel Fitzmaurice

Impí

A ógánaigh,
ná tar i mo dháil,
ná labhair . . .
is binn iad
briathra grá—
is binne aríst
an friotal
nár dúradh ariamh—
níl breith
gan smál—
breith briathar
amhlaidh atá
is ní bheadh ann
ach 'rogha an dá dhíogh'
ó tharla
an scéal mar 'tá . . .

ná bris
an ghloine ghlan
'tá eadrainn
        (ní bristear gloine
        gan fuil is pian)
óir tá Neamh
nó Ifreann thall
'gus cén mhaith Neamh
mura mairfidh sé
go bráth?—
ní Ifreann
go hIfreann
iar-Neimhe . . .

Entreaty

Young man,
do not come near me,
do not speak . . .
the words of love
are sweet—
but sweeter still
is the word
that was never uttered—
no choice
is without stain—
the choice of words
is much the same
and this would be
to choose between evils
in our present
situation . . .

Do not break
the clear glass
between us
        (no glass is broken
        without blood and pain)
for beyond is Heaven
or beyond is Hell
and what good is Heaven
if it is not
for ever?—
the loss of
Heaven
is the worst Hell . . .

impím aríst,
ná labhair,
a ógánaigh,
a 'Dhiarmaid',
is beidh muid
suaimhneach—
an tuiscint do-theangmhaithe
eadrainn
gan gair againn
drannadh leis
le saol na saol
is é dár mealladh
de shíor—
ach impím . . .
ná labhair . . .

I again implore you,
do not speak,
young man,
my 'Diarmaid',
and we will be at peace—
untouchable understanding
between us
we will have no cause
to touch it
ever
as it ever
allures us—
but I implore you . . .
do not speak . . .

Translated by Gabriel Fitzmaurice

PÁDRAIG MAC FHEARGHUSA

Pádraig Mac Fhearghusa was born in Co. Kerry in 1947. Poet, teacher and Irish language activist, his long poem, *Nótaí Treallchogaíochta ó 'Suburbia'*, published in 1983, won the 1982 Open Poetry Award at Writers' Week, Listowel.

Cogar I Leith Chugam

Cogar chugam, a Dhia,
Cén sórt áite é Neamh?
De réir mar a chloisim
Ní réiteodh an áit romhaith liom.

Bheadh sciatháin ar mo dhroim ann,
Is cláireach im ghabháil,
Is mé i mo shuí ar scamall
Ar feadh na gcianta ag seinm stártha.

Sé a deir daoine eile
Nach eol dúinn roimhré
Cad a chífidh súil ann,
Nó cad a bhraithfidh croí.

Ach cogar chugam, a Dhia,
An mbeidh caife ar fáil ar maidin,
Nó piúnt leanna istoíche ann,
Is na haingil, bhfuilid baineann?

Come Here, I Want to Tell You!

Give us a hint, God,
What kind of place is Heaven?
According to what I hear
The place isn't greatly to my liking.

I'd have wings on my back there,
An armful of a harp,
Sitting on a cloud I'd be
Playing turns for eternities.

Other people say
We do not know beforehand
What eye will see there
Or what heart will feel.

But give us a hint, God,
Will there be coffee in the morning,
Or a pint of beer at night,
And the angels, are they female?

Translated by the author

As *Nótaí Treallchogaíochta Ó 'Suburbia'*

I Shanidar na hIaráice
ag bun sléite Zagros
seasca éigin
míle bliain
ó shin
a cuireadh Neanderthalis.
Táthanna grúnlais,
bláthanna iasainte
a leathadh lena ais,
an feochadán,
an caor fíonúna,
bláth an hocais,
ina mbogha corcra,
gorm, dearg,
buí agus bán,
de luibheanna
cumhra leighis
dá anam.
Go ndéana
gráiníní pailíne
do cholna
ár maoth-thoirchiú,
Go leagamna uainn
ag béal d'uagha
driseacha loiscthe
an chumhachta éidreoraigh,
Go sile
ón ár súil
deor dubh torthach
ar luaithreach liath
ár gciníocha díscithe.

From *Nótaí Treallchogaíochta Ó 'Suburbia'* (*Guerilla Notes from Suburbia*)

In Iraqui Shanidar
beaneath the Zagros mountains
some sixty
thousand
years
ago
Neanderthalis was buried.
Clusters of groundsel,
hyacinth flowers
spread beside him,
thistle,
grape,
and mallow flower,
a bow,
purple and blue,
red, yellow, and white,
of fragrant
healing herbs
for his soul.
Moistly may the pollen grains
of your body
fecundate us,
That we may lay aside
at the mouth of your grave
the scorched briars
of shiftless power,
That from our eye
may fall
a black fertile tear
on the grey ashes
of our tribes consumed.

Translated by the author

As *Nótaí Treallchogaíochta Ó 'Suburbia'*

Is sochraid mé ag gabháil go ciúin thar bráid,
is trost na gcos le hais gach rothar ciúin,
glórtha clog na marbh ar a' ngaoith,
is dord an chóiste thar a' mBeithe anonn.
Meirg-gheata ag gíoscán mé cois abhann,
guaille cromtha mé faoi chónra nua,
gairbhéal faoi chois an saol, is lon ar ghéag,
is méirín púca mé, is carnán cré cois uagha.
Deoirín t'rimithe mé ar leiceann liath,
méara sníofa mé ar phaidrín crua,
is suirplís séidte, is deichniúr mé lem linn,
is creathadh lámh, is focal fáin i gcluais.
Ciaróg faoi dheifir mé a' triall chun áir,
sliosadh sluaiste mé go Lá an Luain,
is bóithrín mé is loitheán ciúin im'lár,
gan 'chéim a dhíbreodh scáil an duaircis uaim.

From *Nótaí Treallchogaíochta Ó 'Suburbia'*
(Guerilla Notes from Suburbia)

I am a funeral passing quietly by,
beside each quiet bike a tramp of feet,
the church bells voice upon the wind,
the murmur of the hearse across the Behy.
A creaking rusty gate am I beside that river,
a shoulder bent beneath a glistening coffin,
the world is gravel underfoot, a bird upon a branch,
and I a foxglove, a mound of graveside clay.
A grey tear am I upon a dried cheek,
wrung fingers upon hard beads,
a decade, a swelling surplice while I live am I,
a hand-shake, a stray word in an ear.
I am a beetle hurrying to destroy,
a slicing spade am I until the Day of Judgement,
a quiet puddle on a quiet boreen
from which no foot-step scatters my gloomy shadow.

Translated by the author

MICHEAL O'SIADHAIL

Micheal O'Siadhail was born in Dublin in 1947. Poet, lecturer, linguist, he has published collections in both Irish and English.

Nugent

Meandar cuidsúlach, puth as aer,
Nóiméad é as nuaíocht an lae
Ag léimt thar lampa draíocht
Na teilifíse—an príosúnach.
Th'éis dhá bhliain is naoi mí
Saoradh an príosúnach Nugent inniu
As géibheann na Cise Fada.
                     A Thiarna, ab í
An scéin ag damhsa ina shúile a bhain
Dhár lúdracha muid?
                  Leanadh don stair:
Le scéal eile as Nicearagua,
An rása deiridh as Nás na Rí.
Cén spás atá ag nuaíocht nó ag stair?

Mar sin é. Amáireach feicfear
A pheictiúr ar leithmhilliún páipéar:
Nugent an priosúnach a saoradh inné.
Amáireach tá an seomra thiar le réiteach.

202

Nugent

Eyecatching jiffy, whiff from the sky,
A moment from the news of the day
Darts over the television's
Magic lamp—the prisoner.
Two years nine months after
Prisoner Nugent today released
From Long Kesh camp.
                              God
Was it fright's dance in the eyes
Unhinged us?
                    History continued:
From Nicaragua a news story,
The last race from Naas.
What space has news or history?

That's the way. Tomorrow will see
On a half million newspapers his picture.
Nugent the prisoner yesterday freed.
Tomorrow the backroom must be put in order.

what's the use of principle?

Is amhlaidh a clúdaíodh a shamhail
Le scuaid den phéint.
Cén chúis is fiú snig fola
Gan trácht ar bhláth na hóige;
Le cúrsaí reatha an anama an ceol.

'Sea, cé a bhí i Nugent?
Máirtíreach as an ísealtír
Coipthe ag cúis is ag cearta
Cromtha faoina dhá bhliain fhichead.
Fós in uafás shúile Nugent
Siúileann an saighdiúr singil deiridh
Stiúgtha, stróicthe i ndiaidh Napoleon;
Is 'chuile chúlmhuintir ariamh ag spágáil,
Ag cúitiú dhúinne ár gcompóirte,
Thrí fhearann fuar na staire.
Ab iad a shúile glórach féin
A chuir an scéin seo ionainn?

Actually his image was covered over
By a spatter of paint.
What cause is worth a tint of blood
Not to mind the bloom of youth;
To the soul's current affairs belongs music.

Yes, who was Nugent?
A martyr from the netherland
Feverish with cause and dues
Stooped under twenty two years.
But in the fear of Nugent's eye
Walks the last private soldier
Famished, bedraggled after Napoleon;
All camp followers who ever tramped,
Smarting for our comfort,
Across the cold land of history.
Were those his own crazed eyes
Who terrified us so?

Translated by the author

Ingebjoerg

Cuimhnigh ort féin nach raibh a fhios
Do leithéide go fiú's a bheith ann—
Ach siúd inár láthair de léim thú
I do phatairín gleoite linbh.
Is thú ansin fós i do mháistreás
Gan aird agat ar áit ná ar aimsir,
Goirim is coisricim thú, a shumaigh
'Mór an spóirt thú, a Ingebjoerg.'

I do shúilesa feicim an criostal
I mo chuidsa a facthas tráth—
Cé na tíreacha sin a shiúlfaí,
Cé liachtaí uair i ngrá?
A Ingebjoerg leatsa a labhraím
Teanga nach dtuigfidh tú choíchin,
Gan agam dháiríre le rá leat
Ach gur charaid chaoin í do mháthair.

Ingebjoerg

Just imagine not knowing
The likes of you existed—
But here you spring on us,
Beautiful plump child.
Still a sovereign mistress
Careless of place or time—
I name, bless you, roly-poly
Aren't you lovely Ingebjoerg!

In your eyes I gaze a crystal
The same once seen in mine—
What lands will you travel—
How often fall in love?
Ingebjoerg, I speak with you
A language you won't understand
With only this to tell you—
Your mother was a gentle friend.

Translated by the author

Comaoin

Bhí na mná ariamh uiríseal
A chuir an cogar úd i gcluais an fhir
Gur fireannach gaisciúil é Rí na nDúl
Ach tá fhios againne níos fearr.

I measc mhná na cruinne gile
Casadh corrbhandia i mo bhealach
Aníos thríd an scafall sealadach
A tóigeadh idir am is spás.

Chuir na mná a gcomhairle in éindí,
Mná seo na cruinne gile,
Tharraing beirt nó thriúr an snáth le chéile
Is shníomh siad dhomsa léine.

Mo léine álainn, mo léine féin,
Mo phearsantacht phíosáilte, mo dhán breac,
An léine is goire ná an craiceann
A bhronn mná na cruinne orm.

Compliment

Women were ever humble
Who whispered in the ear of man
That creation's Lord is a swaggering male—
We, of course, know better.

Among the bright world's women
The occasional Goddess came up my way
Through the temporary scaffold elevated
In between time and space.

These women their counsel took
These women of the bright world,
Two or three drew the thread together
And wove for me a shirt

My wonderful shirt, my own shirt
My patchwork self, my motley poem,
The shirt that is nearer to the bone
By the bright world's women endowed.

Translated by the author

An t-Othar

'*An buachaill*' a dúirt muid i gcogar,
Le dochar a bhaint as aineolas
'*An buachaill*', *an portán féin?*

Ó scil ar an meascán suarach
De réasún ruaimneach is de chuisle
Is intinn dhúinn anois é.

Scrúdaigh muid ina shúil an scéin
Lé rún an othair a léamh
Meas tú an bhfuil a fhios aige é?

An bhfuil a fhios aige i measc
Seala banaltraí le gáirí
Geala mar ghiobógaí lín

Gur aingle iad á fhosaíocht
Nach giollaí Pharthais iad
Ach geatóirí ar Gheitseimine?

Bogann an croí seo le truaí
Cruaíonn roimh ghoirm na gcoileach—
Gairdín aonraic é Geitseimine.

Leánn aon deáshamhradh amháin
Cuimhne gach dubhgheimhreadh anall—
Báifear an brón san ádh.

Cascairt na péine an t-áthas;
Go teann i mbéal na scéine
Adhrtar an scéim ina hiomlán.

Patient

'*It is*', we whispered,
Lightening the unlightenment,
'*It is the crab!*'

He's past the paltry skill
Of vein and muddy reason
We name the mind.

Fathoming the unsaid,
We scan terror in his eye
Do you think he knows?

Knows amidst the bevies
Of nurses with light laughter
Gay and white as linen

Knows these guarding angels
Are no paradise messengers
But gate-keepers of Gethsemane

Knows heart moved to pity
Hardens before cock-crow—
Gethsemane is a lonely garden.

One summer will melt
Memories of winter dark:
Our sorrow drowns in luck

As pain must thaw to joy;
Brave in the jaws of terror
We worship the overall.

Translated by the author

Gaineamh

Gaineamh atá san aimsir
Ar ghrinneall abhann.
Thall tá fir an ghaisce
Ag glaomaireacht is ag feadaíl;
I bhfus na mná ag cogarnaíl
Na sciortaí síoda ag priosarnaíl
Thar an uisce anonn.

Tá tuiscint ann nach dtuigtear,
Tobar nach féidir a thomhais,
Go dtiocfaidh bláth bán ar airne
An lá inné ar ais.

Tobar beannaithe na féile
Toil na mná don ghrá;
Billeoig bháite ar a bharr
An cion gágach fireann.

Féachadh tráth lena thomhais
Ach roghar dúinn féin a bhí
Ár scáile umhal féin a facthas—
Tá an tobar seo gan tóin.

Gaineamh atá san aimsir
In intinn an leannáin
Athchiorclaítear aois is óige
Póstar athuair gné is ábhar,
Nua as an bpíosa, nua ón snáth;
Tá an saol aríst ina ghasúr
Is an gaineamh ina am.

Sand

masc/fem

Time is sand
On a river bed
On the far side blustering men
Boast and whistle;
On this side the women whisper
Their silk skirts rustle
Over the water.

There is an understanding not perceived,
A well that cannot be sounded,
Until the sloe blooms white
And yesterday returns.

Woman's will to love
Is a holy well of plenty
A water-lily leaf on its surface
Is the shallow share of the male.

There was an attempt to sound it once
But it was too close to us
We saw our own humble reflection -
This well is bottomless.

Time is sand
In the lover's mind
Age and youth are recircled
Form and substance remarried,
Brand-new, split-new;
The world is a youth again
And sand is time.

Translated by the author

Breaclach

Gluaiseann na sluaite leo is fágann
Ina ndiaidh an fuíoll mar bhotún staire
Le aithrist ortha feasta i meon is i ngnás;
Clár a leasa, dar leo, a bheith dhá réir.
Breac áirithe é an fealsamh ar deoraíocht
Díleachta aimsire idir dhá cheann an mheá
Gan ceann faoi is fós gan tóigeáil a chinn
Ag scríobadh a scéil go ciúin i gcéir a anama.

Ach b'fhéidir gur hiomaí sin babhta cheana
A scalladh gan choinne léas caol an léargais
Ar bhuilcín corr dítreabhach san Éigipt fadó,
Ar mhanach tuata thiar ag tóigeáil scrathógaí
Ar bhreaclach fhuar in Árainn nó Sceilig Mhíchíl.
Cá bhfios nár aimsigh snáthaid chaol an tsolais
An ceol úd ag seinnim i gcéir a n-anama
Scód go scriúta, sheol na sluaite leo.

Stony Patch

The crowds move on and leave
After them the remnants as history's blunder
To mimic them in mind and manner;
Their welfare, they say, to be as them.
A peculiar fish is the philosopher in exile
An orphan of time in the balance
Without bowed head or yet head on high
Scratching his story in the wax of his soul.

But maybe many's the time before
The thin beam of insight was flashed out of
      the blue
On some odd posse of hermits in Egypt long ago,
On a laymonk gathering dungcakes in the west
On a cold stony patch in Aran or Skellig Rock.
How can we know the fine needle of light
      didn't catch
In their soul's wax that music playing?
Sheet to shroud, the crowds sailed on.

Translated by the author

AOGÁN Ó MUIRCHEARTAIGH

Born in Port Laoise in 1948 and reared in Dublin, Aogán Ó Muircheartaigh now lives in the West Kerry Gaeltacht where he is a broadcaster with Raidío na Gaeltachta. His collection of poetry, *Oíche Ghréine*, was awarded the Seán Ó Ríordáin Prize at the 1987 Oireachtas.

Ár nDán

An oíche úd
Gur luíomar
Chun a chéile
Le póg as uaigneas
Nascamar.
Mhaidhm ár ndaonnacht
Eadrainn,
Leáigh dúnéalta
Na gruama
'S do dhein
Oíche ghréine.

Our Fate

That night
We lay
To one another
With a kiss born in loneliness
And we entwined.
Our humanity exploded
Between us
The black clouds of depression
Melted
And it was
A night that the sun shone.

Translated by the author

GABRIEL ROSENSTOCK

Gabriel Rosenstock was born in Kilfinane, Co. Limerick in 1949. He was converted from English to Irish at University College Cork, and became fully initiated in the Kerry Gaeltacht. Poet, playwright, children's author, broadcaster and journalist, his first collection, *Susanne sa Seomra Folctha* (1973), was described by Seán Ó Ríordáin in the *Irish Times* as 'Satanic'. He is one of the most prolific of the poets included in this anthology.

Ravi Shankar

Glaonn

Tú

Anuas

Ó

Na spéartha

Chugainn

Ealaí

Is druideanna

Ravi Shankar

You

Call

Down

From

The sky

To us

Swans

And starlings

Tá

An domhan

Ina

Aigéan

Cluichearnachta

Níl

Mórthír

Le fáil . .

Stopann

Anáil.

The world

Is

An ocean

Fluttering

There is

No

Land . . .

Breathing ceases.
Translated by Gabriel
Fitzmaurice

Teilifís
(faoi m'iníon Saffron)

Ar a cúig a chlog ar maidin
Theastaigh an teilifís uaithi.
An féidir argóint le beainín
Dhá bhliain go leith?
Síos linn le chéile
Níor bhacas fiú le gléasadh
Is bhí an seomra préachta.
Gan solas fós sa spéir
Stánamar le hiontas ar scáileán bán.
Anois! Sásta?
Ach chonaic sise sneachta
Is sioraf trid an sneachta
Is ulchabhán Artach
Ag faoileáil
Os a chionn.

Television
(for my daughter Saffron)

At five o'clock in the morning
She wanted television.
Who can argue with a little woman
Two and a half years old?
Down we went together
I didn't even dress
And the room was freezing.
No light yet in the sky
We stared in wonder at the white screen.
Happy now?
But she saw snow
And a giraffe through it
And an arctic owl
Wheeling
Above it.

Translated by Gabriel Fitzmaurice

Billy Holiday

D'fháiscis pian
As sárbhinneas
Binneas
As sárphian
Nuair a éigníodh thú in aois
Do dheich mbliana duit
B'in an chéad tairne
I gcéasadh do chine is do bhanúlachta
Is d'ealaíne
Go dtí sa deireadh
Gur scanraigh do ghuth féin tú,
A ainnir i sról.

Billy Holiday

You squeezed pain
From the height of sweetness
Sweetness
From the height of pain
When you were raped
At ten years old
That was the first nail
In the crucifixion of your race, your womanhood
And your art
Till in the end
Your own voice frightened you
Lady in satin.

Translated by Gabriel Fitzmaurice

Tóraíocht

Cá bhfuil na dánta a gheallas
A scríobhfainn duit?
Nílid i ndúch—
Gheobhair iad i gcúr aibhneacha
I bhfarraigí
I ngal os cionn failltreacha
Ina nguairneáin gaoithe
I súile fiolar
Sna scamaill
Sna spéartha
Fiú sna réalta.
Táid ar a gcúrsa síoraí
Ó neamhní go neamhní.
Nílid i gcló—
Sciob cumhracht bláthanna iad
Is tú ar do ghogaide sa ghairdín,
Ghoin neantóga iad
Chuimil copóga iad
Thuirling bóiní Dé orthu
Is shiúil go criticiúil
Ag cuardach ríme is meadarachta
Gan teacht ar theideal fiú.
Ní féidir tú a ainmniú!
Gairim thú ó lá go lá
le gach anáil.
Cá bhfuil na briathra?
Ghlacais chugat féin iad.
Na haidiachtaí?

The Search
for my wife, Eithne

1

Where are the poems I promised
I would write for you?
They are not in ink—

You will find them in the foam of rivers
In the seas
In the vapour above clifftops
In the swirling breeze
In eagles' eyes
In the clouds
In the skies
Even in the stars.
They're on their eternal journey
From void to void.
They are not in print—
The flowers' sweetness snatched them
While you hunkered in the garden.
Nettles burned them
Dock soothed them
Ladybirds landed on them
And walked like critics
Seeking rhyme and metre.
They even failed to find a title. For who
Could put a name on you!
And yet each day I name you
With every breath.
Where are all the verbs?
You have gathered them to yourself.
The adjectives?

Neadaoínn id bhrollach geal.
Poncaíocht?
Tá tú maisithe aici,
Ainmfhocail, gutaí is consain,
Nathanna uile na Gaeilge
Tiomnaím duit iad—Eithne!

ll
Ó aois go haois lorgaím do chló
I m'eite
Im dhuilleog,
Nuair is leanaí sinn
Laochra
Seanóirí,
Ar lic an bháis
Is fiú sa bhroinn
Tá gach nóiméad le saol na saol
Ag ullmhú dom dhánsa duit—
Ag cur fáilte romhat.
An gcloisir gála?
Casann an domhan
Casann gach ní
Casann na cnoic is na sléibhte.
Dhúnamar, d'osclaíomar ár súile
Is dhún arís le hiontas.

Nestling in your breast.
Punctuation?
It adorns you.
Nouns, vowels, consonants,
The Irish language, its sound and sense,
I dedicate to you, Eithne.

11
From age to age I seek your shape
Like a winglet
Like a leaf.
When we are children,
Heroes
And elders,
On death's cold stone
And in the womb,
Every moment
Shapes my poem—
It ever welcomes you.
Can you hear the gale?
The world turns
And all is turning,
The hills and the peaks above them.
We closed our eyes, and opened them,
Then closed them again in wonder.

lll

Ná beannaigh dom
Ná féach orm
Ná lorg mé
Táim ar mo theitheadh
Ad lorg
Ní hann dúinn
Áit ar bith
Am ar bith,
Nílimid i bhfriotal
Nílimid i ngrá
(Dá dhéine ár ngrá dá chéile).
Beir ar lámh orm,
A chuisle; éist le tiompán an chroí
A bhuail dúinn anallód,
Ní thuigimid fós a bhrí.

lll

Do not greet me
Do not look at me
Do not seek me
I escape
I seek you
We do not exist
In any time
In any place
We are not in the realms of words
Or love
(Although our love is strong).
Take my hand,
Love; hear the heart's tympany
That beat long ago for you and me,
That we still don't understand.

Translated by Gabriel Fitzmaurice

Uaireanta Is Fear Bréige Mé

1

Uaireanta is fear bréige mé,
Scanraím mé féin—
Céasann mo bhréaga féin mé.

Bain mo chuid éadaí díom
Srac as a chéile iad
Cuir m'ionathar trí thine
Go gcloise mé scréach péine
Mo bhreithe.
Shiúlfainn tríd an saol ansin im bhladhm
Labhróinn i dteangacha tine
Dhéanfainn damhsa ag aontaí
Scanróinn páistí
Cad nach ndéanfainn!
Lingeadh san aer im chaor aduaidh
Im réalta reatha trí Bhealach na Bó Finne.
Uaireanta is fear bréige mé,
Scanraím mé féin—
Céasann mo bhréaga féin mé.

ll

Tagadh an fiach dubh
Piocadh sé na súile asam
Dhéanfainn gáire dubh dóite ag bainis
Thabharfainn léim as mo chraiceann
        ag baisteadh
D'íosfainn an féar glas!
D'ólfainn mún an ghiorria!
Is fear bréige mé
Idir neamh agus talamh
Dall ar mo chinniúint

Sometimes I'm a Phoney Man

l

Sometimes I'm a phoney man,
I frighten myself—
My lies crucify me.

Strip me of my clothes
Tear them asunder
Burn my entrails
Until I hear my own
Birth-cry.
I would walk the world then, a flame,
I would talk in tongues of fire,
I would dance at fairs
I would frighten children
What wouldn't I do!
I would leap in the air like the northern lights
Like stars running through the Milky Way.
Sometimes I'm a phoney man,
I frighten myself—
My lies crucify me.

ll

Let the raven come
Let him pick my eyes out
I would laugh a black scorched laugh at a wedding
    feast
I would jump out of my skin at a baptism
I would eat the green grass:
I would drink hare's piss!
I am a phoney man
Between heaven and earth
Blind to destiny

Ní fios mo ghinealach
As foirnéis m'anama
Éalaíonn splancacha
Trím shúil.
Uaireanta is fear bréige mé,
Scanraím mé féin—
Céasann mo bhréaga féin mé.

lll

Ní cás liom an cloigeann seo
A thuilleadh—
Fág orm an hata, ámh,
Rachainn faoi lámh an easpaig
Bhainfinn na fáinní dá mhéara
Cheannóinn roinnt builíní aráin
Móide dhá iasc leasaithe
Is d'fhanfainn le míorúilt
Nó go mbeinn stiúgtha.
Uaireanta is fear bréige mé,
Scanraím mé féin—
Céasann mo bhréaga féin mé.

lV

Cé a leath tarra ar mo theanga
Agus cleití?
Fastaoim!
Labhróidh an ghaoth tríom
De shíor
As gach aird
Scéalta seaca
Lucht taistil
Scéalta na dteifeach is na bpobal gan díon.
Uaireanta is fear bréige mé,
Scanraím mé féin—
Céasann mo bhréaga féin mé.

Ignorant of pedigree
From the furnace of my soul
Sparks escape
Through my eyes.
Sometimes I'm a phoney man,
I frighten myself—
My lies crucify me.

lll

This skull doesn't concern me
Any more—
Leave my hat on, however,
I would be confirmed
I would take the rings from the Bishop's fingers
I would buy some loaves of bread
And two cured fish
And would await the miracle
Until perished with hunger and thirst.
Sometimes I'm a phoney man,
I frighten myself—
My lies crucify me.

IV

Who tarred and feathered
My tongue?
Hold fast!
The wind will speak through me
Ceaselessly
From every quarter
In the forgotten tales
Of travellers
Fugitives' stories, stories of a roofless people.
Sometimes I'm a phoney man,
I frighten myself—
My lies crucify me.

V

Iompair chun na habhann mé
Abhainn na Bóinne
An Níl
Tum sa Ghanga mé
Nó in Abhainn na hIordáine:
Thaistilíos trí thine
Trí dhíseart
Is thar leac oighir
Im dhícheannach dílis
Dar Duach!
Éilím faoi dheoidh bruach!

V

Take me to the river
The Boyne
The Nile
Immerse me in the Ganges
Or in the River Jordan:
I travelled through fire
Through desert
And through ice
Headless, faithful
By God
I demand to be taken to the brink.

Translated by Gabriel Fitzmaurice

DEAGLÁN COLLINGE

Deaglán Collinge was born in Dublin in 1949. Poet, teacher, broadcaster and part-time lecturer, he has a PhD on the works of Máirtín Ó Direáin. He writes both in Irish and English.

Aingeal an Uabhair

Gnúiseanna corraithe a gcairde
I bhfáinne bailithe
Ag deireadh ré:
Solas gorm bladhmach
Ag sméideadh báis nó beatha
Is an marcach óg faoi chóta
A chapall mire sractha
A chlogad crua daite
Nár mhaolaigh luas a bheatha
Scoilte . . .

Cuirfidh bás an taoisigh
Srian le luas na n-aingeal;
Ach go fealltach formhothaithe
Bíogfaidh sé chun beatha,
Líonfar an folús,
Is cuirfidh drithlín ghluaiseachta
Ainmneacha eile
De shíor i leabhar.

Fallen Angel

His friends' faces moving,
Close in a circle
At the end of his era:
The blue blinding bulb
Flashing life or death,
And a coat
Covering the young rider,
His wild steed torn asunder,
The tough coloured helmet
That failed to stem
His life's full speed,
Cracked . . .

The leader's death
Will slow the angels' flight;
But treacherously,
And imperceptibly,
Life will kick again.
The vacuum will be filled,
And the thrill of movement
Will number other names,
Ceaselessly.

Translated by the author

Féileacán Cabáiste

A chliúsaí chaoil,
Ag leathadh sciathán mín
Náiríonn tú glan
An caisearbhán gairéadach
A umhlaíonn cromtha fút:

Ar chóir mar sin
Gur rith sé liom
An gas cabáiste claon
Pollta stróicthe lom
Ag craos do chnuimhe glaise?

Gan chnuimh sa tsrón
Agam duit fín,
Is buan an t-ábhar machnaimh é:
An milleann gach rud álainn
Nó an meath an áille féin?

Large White Cabbage Butterfly

Stretching a powdered delicate
Wing, slim coquette
You shame the garish dandelion
With beauty in perfection:

What made me think
Of one remaining cabbage stalk
Perforated, useless, torn
By slimy gobs of green?

Conceited mind fluttering toward
Food for thought,
Do all things beautiful corrupt,
Or is corruption beauty in a word?

Translated by the author

Báisteach

Giob geab báistí amuigh
A scaipeann tromluí orm
I gciúnas oíche:

B'fhada spalladh triomaigh
An glas go feo
De réir a chéile,
Buíochan ar ghnúiseanna
Is craiceann ag scamhadh
Ar ócáidí,
De thaisme.

Anois an bháisteach fhionnuar
I gcaisí síodacha
Anuas orainn
Ag scaoileadh ghreim na meirbhe
Is fáiltím roimh a teacht
Mar a d'fháilteoinn
Roimh *détente*,
A scaipfeadh tromluí
Ar m'intinn
De bháisteach dhubh
Is craiceann scafa
Is cat mara anuas orainn uile
De thaisme.

Rain

The babbling rain outside
Dissipates my nightmare
In the night's tranquillity:

Long was the arid spell
Green browning gradually
Faces bronzing
And skin peeling
On occasion
Accidentally.

Now the soothing rain
Plashes round us
In silken torrents
Breaking the spell of drought
And I welcome its arrival
As I would *détente*
To dissipate the nightmare
From my mind
Of blackening rain
And skin peeling
And apocalypse on all of us
Accidentally.

Translated by the author

Ménage à Trois

Mar stuaic thriantáin chomhshleasaigh
A uilleacha géar chun stróicthe
Ba mhian leis sleasa breise.

Níl tairiscint ag bun triantáin
Do bhean amháin ag fanacht
Go himníoch le comhroinnt.

Scóladh croí i ndeireadh lae
An chruabhreith á léamh
'Is mó aon dá thaobh tríantáin
Ná an tríú taobh.'

Ménage à Trois

Heading the isosceles triangle
Its razor angles set to tear
He seeks to run from his affair.

Neither woman wanting base
Waiting for an option
Fearing full bisection.

Heartscald in the courtroom
The geometric word:
'Any two sides of a triangle
Are greater than a third.'

Translated by the author

An Fiolar Maol
(Siombal shaoirse Mheiriceá)

Teanntaithe in éanadán gránna
Grinnsúile nimhneacha
Doiléir le tean éadóchais,
Ag síneadh sciatháin chumasaigh
Os comhair an tsaoil,
Do sheas an fiolar maol:

Ar ais nó ar éigean
Bhí an tsaoirse féin i ngéibheann
Is ina háit rud déistineach
Go bagarthach urchóideach.

Ní beo an fiolar fágtha mar atá
Ach an mbeadh sé baileach fíor a rá,
Go deo nach sroisfeadh sé
An spéir, dá scaoilfí é?

(Gairdín na n-ainmhithe, Philadelphia)

The Bald Eagle
(The Freedom Symbol of America)

There in its monstrous cage
Sharp eyes dim with despair,
Stretching a powerful wing,
The bald eagle:

Nor could I but envisage
Liberty incarcerated there
And in its place a monstrous thing
Strikingly a symbol:

If left the bald eagle must die
If freed, could the bird fly?

(Philadelphia Zoo)
Translated by the author

Rún Na Striapaí

'Scríobhfaidh mé scéal mo bheatha',
Arsa an striapach lá,
'Is leis an bhfáltas
Mairfidh mé go cuibhiúil feasta.'

Ar an bpointe, chroith bunchloch
Clainne stáit is eaglaise
Is níor dhúthrachtaí paidir
An fhir chlainne is an pholaiteora
Ar a nglúine
Ná achainí an easpaig
Ag umhlú os cionn na maighdine:
Mar ó rinne sí súgán díobh
Ní dea-chlú go súgán sneachta
I mbéal striapaí.

The Harlot's Secret

I shall write the story of my life,
Said the harlot one day,
And with the proceeds
Shall live respectably
In future.

On the instant the cornerstone
Of family church and state
Trembled loudly
And no more earnest
Was the prayer of family man
And politician on their knees
Than the pleading
Of the bishop
Crouched low before the Virgin
For once around her finger
What was social status but a puff of smoke
From a harlot's mouth?

Translated by the author

Coscairt Earraigh

Fáiscthe le chéile
Ar shleasa Loch Bré,
Do bhraitheamar léirscrios oighir
Le cianta cairbreacha:
Fánaí cruinne, talamh méith,
Scríobtha lom gan bhrí,
Fásach éibhir ag fógairt
Chosc na mblianta:

Ach thuas ar stuaic Chipiúir
Do sheas ga borb gréine
Ag sá na spéartha sléibhe:
Do chorraigh fathach as a shuan
Is theannas i do ghaire,
Deireadh troda feicthe agam
Sa loinnir i do shúile.

Spring Thaw

Huddled together at Lough Bray,
We saw the ruin
Of centuries of ice:
Rounded slopes once teeming
Scoured and stripped of life,
Barren granite screaming
Aeons of inhibition:

But from above Kippure
A shaft of sun was piercing
Mountain skies,
A sleeping giant was stirring
And I held you, feeling sure
The melt of long resistance started
From the promise of your eyes.

Translated by the author

MICHAEL DAVITT

Michael Davitt was born in Cork city in 1950. He graduated from University College Cork, with a degree in Celtic Studies in 1971. Poet, broadcaster and editor of *Innti*, which is, more than any, the magazine of contemporary poetry in the Irish language.

Poker

Nach ceait mar atá
ag deireadh an lá
tar éis grá
na gaoithe binbeach.

D'imigh sí uait
is d'fhág sí tú
gan phunt
gan tuiseal ginideach.

Poker

Isn't it cat, my friend,
at the day-end
after love
like a wind that's venomous

She's left and gone
and here I am
flat broke
without a genitive.

Translated by Gabriel Fitzmaurice

Do Bhobby Sands An Lá Sular Éag Sé

Fanamaid,
mar dhaoine a bheadh
ag stánadh suas
ceithre urlár ar fhear
ina sheasamh ar leac fuinneoige
ag stánadh anuas orainn
go tinneallach.

Ach an féinmharú d'íobairtse?
ní géilleadh, ní faoiseamh;
inniu ní fiú rogha duit
léimt nó gan léimt.

Nílimid cinnte
dár bpáirtne sa bhuile;
pléimid ceart agus mícheart
faoi thionchar ghleo an tí óil;
fanaimid ar thuairiscí nua,
ar thuairimí nua *video*.

Fanaimid, ag stánadh,
inár lachain i gclúmh sóch,
ar na cearca sa lathach
is an coileach ag máirseáil thart
go bagarthach ar a ál féin,
ar ál a chomharsan
is i nguth na poimpe glaonn:
'coir is ea coir is ea coir.'

For Bobby Sands on the Day Before he Died

We wait
like people
staring up
four floors at a man
standing on a windowsill
who is staring down at us
nervously.

But is your sacrifice suicide?
it is not surrender, it is not release;
today you haven't even the choice
of jumping or not.

We're not certain
of our part in this madness;
we wrangle over right and wrong
when our blood's up in the pub;
we wait for the latest bulletins
the latest videoed opinions.

We wait, staring,
like ducks in cosy plumage,
at the hens in the mire
while the cock struts
threateningly around his own brood
and his neighbours'
pompously crowing:
'A crime is a crime is a crime.'

militancy
of gov.

Thit suan roimh bhás inniu ort.
Cloisimid ar an raidió
glór do mhuintire faoi chiach,
an chumha ag sárú ar an bhfuath:
is é ár nguí duit
go mbuafaidh.

You fell into a death-sleep today.
We hear on the radio
the catch in the voice of your people,
sorrow overwhelming hate:
our prayer for you
is that it will.

Translated by Gabriel Fitzmaurice

Ragham Amú
do Ghabriel

Is bás, dar liom fós, freagairt,
Is beatha fiafraí -
Ragham amú tamall eile
Is chífeam an tír.
                    —*Seán Ó Ríordáin*

ragham amú
siar ó dheas
aniar aduaidh
beam ag tnúth
le teas an ghutha
ragham ag triall
ar Rí na bhFeart
is i ndeasghnáth
coinnle is craicinn
i gCaiseal Mumhan
dófam ár seascdhámh
i dtine chnámh
is scaipfeam an luaith
ar choincleach an traidisiúin
ragham amú
déanfam dearmhad
ar mhórdhearmhad
i seachrán sléibhe
nó ar maos
sa riasc
idir Altán Mór
is Altán Beag
ag stáisiún traenach
Chaiseal na gCorr

We Will Stray
for Gabriel

Answering, I still think, is death
Life is question -
We will stray another while
And see the land
                    —*Séan Ó Ríordáin*

We will stray
south-west by south
from the north-west
we will expect the heat of voice
we will seek Almighty God
and the rite
of candles and skin
in Cashel
we will singe our barren bards
in a bonfire
and scatter their ashes
on the mildew of tradition
we will stray
we will make mistake
upon mistake
in our mountain wandering
or steeped
in a marsh
between
Altán Mór
and Altán Beag
at the railway station
of Caiseal na gCorr

fágfam slán
leis an traein stairiúil
a théann amú
ragham amú
ag guthántaíocht
ó pholla go polla
i gcearnóga feinistreacha
Bhleá Cliath a dó
go loiscfear sinn
i ndeargchogar
an ghutha mhóir
tabharfam timchuairt
na himpireachta lathaí
ar ghlúine gágacha
ag gairm go hard
na máistrí
Ó Bruadair
Eoghan Rua
Aodhagán
cuirfeam dínn
an cian oidhreachtúil
is ragham amú
tá an guth
ag tuar ré nua
ré an duine bhig
ré an tsaoil istigh
ré an tSasanaigh
ré an Eireannaigh
ré na bprátaí úra
sáfam biorán suain
i gcroí an bhuama
ár gceann i súil
an hairicín

we will bid farewell
to the historic train
that goes astray
we will stray
phoning
from poll to poll
in the windowed squares
of Dublin two
until we are burnt
in the bloody whisperings
of the great voice
we will force a circuit
of the muddy empire
on chafed knees
calling loudly on
the masters
Ó Bruadair
Eoghan Rua
Aodhagán
we will banish
the hereditary depression
and we will stray
the voice
is heralding a new age
the age of the small man
the age of the inner life
the age of the English
the age of the Irish
the age of new potatoes
we will anaesthetise
the heart of the bomb
our head in the eye
of the hurricane

canfam roscanna breithe
roscanna fáis
ní dhamnóm
ach Ainglin an Uabhair
daonnóm an Eaglais
cuirfeam deireadh
le mór is fiú
ragham amú
is i ndeireadh
an chúrsa thiar
mairfeam faoi adhall
ag cur tráthnóntaí
píopaí cré amú
ag claochlú
claochlóm
ragham uasal
ragham íseal
éireom

we will sing birth-songs
growing songs
we will condemn only
the Angel of Pride
we will humanise the Church
we will end
conceit
we will stray
and at the end
of the day
we will live in heat
sending evenings
of clay pipes astray
changing
we will change
we will go proud
we will go low
we will go

Translated by Gabriel Fitzmaurice

Urnaí Maidne

Slogann dallóg na cistine a teanga de sceit
caochann an mhaidin liathshúil.
Seacht nóiméad déag chun a seacht
gan éan ar chraobh
ná coileach ag glaoch
broidearnach im shúil chlé
is blas bréan im bhéal.

Greamaíonn na fógraí raidió den bhfo-chomhfhios
mar a ghreamódh
buíocán bogbheirithe uibh
de chois treabhsair dhuibh
mar a ghreamódh cnuimh de chneá.
Ná héisteodh sibh
in ainm dílis Dé *ÉISTÍG*...

Tagann an citeal le blubfhriotal miotalach
trí bhuidéal bainne ón gcéim
dhá mhuga mhaolchluasacha chré.
Dúisigh a ghrá
tá sé ina lá. Seo, cupán tae
táim ag fáil bháis
conas tánn tú fhéin?

Morning Prayer

The kitchen blind swallows its tongue in fright
morning winks a grey eye.
Seventeen minutes to seven
no bird on a branch
and no cock crowing
a throbbing in my left eye
and a foul taste in my mouth.

The radio ads cling to the unconscious
as the yolk
of a soft-boiled egg
would cling to a black trousers
as a maggot would cling to a wound.
Listen
in God's name *SHUT UP* . . .

The kettle comes with metallic splutter
three bottles from the doorstep
two abashed clay mugs.
Wake up love
it's day. Here's a cup of tea
I'm dying
how are you?

Translated by Gabriel Fitzmaurice

An Scáthán
i gcuimhne m'athar

I

Níorbh é m'athair níos mó é
ach ba mise a mhacsan;
paradacsa fuar a d'fháisceas,
dealbh i gculaith Dhomhnaigh
a cuireadh an lá dár gcionn.

Dhein sé an-lá deora, seirí,
fuiscí, ceapairí feola is tae.
Bhí seanchara leis ag eachtraí
faoi sciurd lae a thugadar
ar Eochaill sna triochaidí
is gurbh é an chéad pháirtí é
i seirbhís Chorcaí/An Sciobairín
amach sna daicheadaí.
Bhí dornán cártaí Aifrinn
ar mhatal an tseomra suí
ina gcorrán thart ar vás gloine,
a bhronntanas scoir ó C.I.E.

II

Níorbh eol dom go ceann dhá lá
gurbh é an scáthán a mharaigh é . . .

An seanscáthán ollmhór Victeoiriach
leis an bhfráma ornáideach bréagórga
a bhí romhainn sa tigh trí stór
nuair a bhogamar isteach ón tuath.

The Mirror
in memory of my father

I

He was no longer my father
but I was still his son;
I would get to grips with that cold paradox,
the remote figure in his Sunday best
who was buried the next day.

A great day for tears, snifters of sherry,
whiskey, beef sandwiches, tea.
An old mate of his was recounting
their day excursion
to Youghal in the Thirties,
how he was his first partner
on the Cork/Skibbereen route
in the late Forties.
There was a splay of Mass cards
on the sitting-room mantelpiece
which formed a crescent round a glass vase,
his retirement present from C.I.E.

II

I didn't realize till two days later
it was the mirror took his breath away.

The monstrous old Victorian mirror
with the ornate gilt frame
we had found in the three-storey house
when we moved in from the country.

Bhínn scanraithe roimhe: go sciorrfadh
anuas den bhfalla is go slogfadh mé
d'aon tromanáil i lár na hoíche...

Ag maisiú an tseomra chodlata dó
d'ardaigh sé an scáthán anuas
gan lámh chúnta a iarraidh;
ar ball d'iompaigh dath na cré air,
an oíche sin phléasc a chroí.

III
Mar a chuirfí de gheasa orm
thugas faoin jab a chríochnú:
an folús macallach a pháipéarú,
an fhuinneog ard a phéinteáil,
an doras marbhlainne
a scríobadh. Nuair a rugas ar an scáthán
sceimhlíos. Bhraitheas é ag análú tríd.
Chuala é ag rá i gcogar téiglí:
I'll give you a hand, here.

Is d'ardaíomar an scáthán thar n-ais in airde
os cionn an tinteáin,
m'athair á choinneáil
fad a dheineas-sa é a dhaingniú
le dhá thairne.

I was afraid that it would sneak
down from the wall and swallow me up
in one gulp in the middle of the night.

While he was decorating the bedroom
he had taken down the mirror
without asking for help;
soon he turned the colour of terracotta
and his heart broke that night.

III

There was nothing for it
but to set about finishing the job,
papering over the cracks,
painting the high window,
stripping the door, like the door of a crypt.
When I took hold of the mirror
I had a fright. I imagined him breathing through it.
I heard him say in a reassuring whisper:
I'll give you a hand, here.

And we lifted the mirror back in position
above the fireplace,
my father holding it steady
while I drove home
the two nails.

Translated by Paul Muldoon

Cuairt Ar Thigh M' Aintíní An Nollaig Sarar Rugadh Mé

Na ráithí gan mheáchan:
cuachta i mbolglann a tí Shasanaigh.
a croí-bhuillí fó thoinn,
a guth imirceora ag teacht i dtír
ar aiteas na háite.

An Nollaig sarar rugadh mé
bhusamar go léir amach
ar cuairt chuig deirféaracha a céile,
snasairí singile taephotaí airgid
i dtearmann de Valera;
ní foláir nó níor ligeas i ndearmad
an chaint antaiseipteach
sa chistin thílithe,
ná an staighre bog.
Maireann na fasaigh neamh-mhínithe,
na braistintí bheith gafa tríd
sara dtagaim chuige.

Dosaon bliain dom san atmaisféar,
im aoi-*soprano* cúinne sa chistin chéanna
ná hiarrfadh ná diúltódh athchupán
a chaithfeadh amhrán le Thomas Moore
a chanadh, a chaithfeadh aontú
nárbh aon mhaith an Ghaeilge
chun fáil isteach sa Bhanc,
a shleamhnódh amach
an staighre clúmhach suas
chun faoisimh seal ón ngaol-lathas.

Na ráithí suansiúil.

A Visit to my Aunts' House
the Christmas before I was Born

The floating seasons:
crouched in the stomach of her English house,
her underwater heart beats,
her immigrant's voice keeping its head above
the strangeness of the place.

The Christmas before I was born
we all bussed out
on a visit to her spouse's sisters,
two silver tea-pot spinsters
in de Valera's shining sanctuary;
I must never have forgotten
the antiseptic talk
in the tiled kitchen
nor the feel of the soft stairs.
Precedents remain unexplained,
feelings of have gone through it
before I get there.

In twelfth year of atmosphere,
a guest soprano in the corner of that same kitchen,
reluctant to either ask for or refuse another cup,
felt obliged to perform a Thomas Moore song
and agree that Irish would not help
to get a job in the Bank,
would slip out
up the down stairs
for brief relief from relatocracy.

The sleep-walking seasons.

Translated by the author

LIAM Ó MUIRTHILE

Liam Ó Muirthile was born in Cork city in 1950. He works as a journalist and Irish language newsreader for RTE. His first collection, *Tine Chnámh*, (Dublin 1984), was very well received. He won Duais an Ríordánaigh at Oireachtas 1983. In 1984 he was given the Irish American Cultural Institute Award.

Do Chara Liom

Bhí d'fhéasóg riamh ciardhubh trom;
Maidin in óstán i nGaillimh chomhairlís dom
An fás saonta ar m'aghaidh féin
A bhogadh amach ar dtúis le huisce
Sula raghainn á bhearradh le lann.
Tá tú anois briste, ar bhinse i ndump daonna
Mar sheantreabhsar caite i gcúinne i ndearmad.
Is é do dhoircheacht is túisce a thagann chun mo
	chuimhne
San ospidéal, tráthnóna rothaíochta ar cuairt;
Is náiríonn mo bheith chomh mór le chéile mé i do
	láthair,
Tá na hothair ag imirt leadóg bhoird le do smionaga
	cinn
Tá pána amháin ar iarraidh sa bhfuinneog
	choirceogach
Is cuireann othar ina dhrárs gach cúpla nóiméad a
	lámh amach tríd.

For a Friend

Your beard was always thick and jet-black.
You advised me one morning in a Galway hotel
To soften the boyish growth of my own face
With water before shaving with a blade.

You are broken now on a bench in a human heap
Like old trousers left in a corner, forgotten.
It is your darkness which first strikes me
On an afternoon bicycle visit to the hospital.

My togetherness shames me in your presence.
Patients are playing ping-pong with your brains.
A pane of glass is missing from a hive-shaped
        window
And an inmate in drawers sticks his hand through
        it intermittently.

Is deireann tú féin go mbraitheann tú uait Beethoven,
Ní ligfidh siad amach ag siúl sinn sa ghairdín—
Tá eagla orthu go n-éireoidh na bláthanna
      scitsifréineach
Is go mbéicfidh siad ar Wordsworth in ard a gcinn—
Is náirím arís nuair a deireann tú go fírinneach
Gur mhaith leat go bhfaighinn pianó duit i dtigh
      na ngealt
Chun go bhféadfá do laethanta a thabhairt ag
      méirínteacht
Ar na nótaí ciúine uafáis in *soledad*.

You mention that you miss Beethoven.
They say we cannot go into the garden.
They are terrified the flowers will turn
    schizophrenic
And commence howling for Wordsworth.

I am ashamed again when you say in all sincerity
That you'd like me to get you a piano into the
    mad-house,
So you could pass your days tinkering with the
    quiet notes
Of terror in *soledad*.

Translated by Greg Delanty

Mise

Díothódsa tusa fós i m'aigne,
A bhean na beagmhaitheasa,
Ach tógann sé tamall an dealg nimhe
A chuir tú ionam a tharraingt go hiomlán;
Ba dhóbair duit mé scrios gan oiread
Is súil a chaochadh le trócaire;
Agus cé go ndeirtear gur deacair
An croí a chneasú nuair a lúbtar
Cuimhním ar shamhail an rotha chairte
A dheineadh m'athair aimsir an Chogaidh
Is é ag rá: 'leamhán sa stoc, dair sna spócaí,
Agus leamhán arís amuigh sa bhfonsa.'
San áit a ndeisídís iad i gCorcaigh
Chaithidís dul leis an snáithe
Is an dair a scoilteadh le tua.
Bíse id dhair anois agus scoiltfead
Tú ó bhun go barr leis an gceardaíocht
Is dual dom mhuintir, ainm nach
Bhféadfása is tú den stoc gur díobh tú
A litriú: Ó Muirthile Carraige.

Me

I'll annihilate you yet from my mind,
Woman of little worth,
But it takes time
To withdraw your venomous dart.
You near destroyed me
Without a sliver of sympathy.

I fall back on the image of the cartwheel
My father made in Cork during the war
And him saying: 'Elm in the shaft, oak in the spokes
And elm again in the rim.'
They had to go with the grain
And split the oak with an axe.

And though it's said to be difficult
To mend a broken heart,
Let you now be oak and I'll split you in two
With the craft innate to my people,
Whose name, given your stock,
You couldn't even spell: Ó Muirthile Carraige.

Translated by Greg Delanty

Beoldath

Go dtí go bhfaca tú
Shamhlaíos beoldath leis na Caogadaí,
Smearadh smeachta tapaidh roimh aifreann an
    Domhnaigh,
Deabhadh amach ar mo mháthair go ceann a
    dódhéag;
Ach an rud a mharaíodh ar fad mé
Sna sála uirthi suas Sráid na Dúglaise,
An díriú fústrach sa tsiúl di ar a stocaí níolóin
An fhéachaint siar thar ghualainn ar na huaimeanna
Is d'fhiafraínn ionam féin cár chuadar, cár chuadar?
Thóg sé i bhfad orm ach táim tagtha aisti,
Ag dul i bhfeabhas, ag téarnamh is dóigh liom;
Tar éis duit an phóg bhinn amháin sin a thabhairt
    dom
Led liopaí nuamhaisithe lonrach;
Baineann milseacht anois le beoldath,
Díreach milseacht aeróbach.

Lipstick

Until I saw you
I associated lipstick with the fifties;
A smacking daub before mass on Sunday,
My mother in a rush out to the 12 o'clock.
But what killed me altogether,
Hard on her heels up Douglas Street,
Was the agitated glancing over her shoulder
At the seams of her Sunday-morning nylons.

I used to ask myself: Where did they go?
Where did they go?
It took a long time, but I've grown out of that:
Improving, recovering I suppose,
After you gave me that one sweet kiss
With your bright, newly painted lips.
Now I associate lipstick with sweetness;
An airtight sweetness.

Translated by Greg Delanty

Carraig Aifrinn

Seachas dún dúnta na soiniciúlachta
Osclaíonn mo chroí amach
Do gheata cois trá i Maoinis;
Treoraíonn sé go discréideach mé
Isteach in aerspás Chonamara,
Agus san áit nach bhfaca mé féin
Ar chor ar bith
I locha dubha a súl
Faighim cuireadh anois
O gheata adhmaid i Maoinis.
Roinnim libh
Rún ciúin na maidine seo,
Rón muiníneach, ba ar dhuirling.
Is tagann an fharraige
Timpeall na carraige
Mar a scuabfadh sagart
A lámha le chéile
Le linn aifrinn.

Mass Rock

Blinded by the closed fortress of cynicism
My heart opens out
To a gate by the sea at Maoinis;
It guides me without ceremony
Into the Connemara airspace,
And in the place I couldn't see myself
Reflected
In the black lakes of their eyes
I am invited now
By a wooden gate in Maoinis.
I share with you
This morning's gentle secret,
A trusting seal, cows on a stony shore,
And the sea washes
Around the rock
As a priest
Would sweep his hands together
During Mass.

Translated by Gabriel Fitzmaurice

NUALA NÍ DHOMHNAILL

Nuala Ní Dhomhnaill was born in Lancashire in 1952 and grew up in the Kerry Gaeltacht and in Nenagh, Co. Tipperary. She spent seven years wandering in Turkey and Holland and now lives in Dublin with her Turkish husband and four children. She has published two highly acclaimed collections, and has been translated extensively by Michael Hartnett.

Póg

Do phóg fear eile mé
i lár mo bheola,
do chuir sé a theanga
isteach i mo bhéal.
Níor bhraitheas faic.
Dúrt leis
'Téir abhaile, a dheartháirín,
tán tú ólta
is tá do bhean thall sa doras
ag fanacht.'

Ach nuair a chuimhním
ar do phógsa
critheann mo chromáin
is imíonn
a bhfuil eatarthu
ina lacht.

Kiss

Straight on my mouth
another man's kiss.
He put his tongue
between my lips.
I was numb
and said to him
'Little man, go home
you're drunk
your wife waits at the door.'

But when I recall
your kiss
I shake, and all
that lies
between my hips
liquefies
to milk.

                    Translated by Michael Hartnett

Mo Mhíle Stór

I dtús mo shaoil do mheallais mé
i dtráth m'óige, trí mo bhoige.
Thuigis go maith
go bhféadfaí mo cheann a chasadh
le trácht ar chúirteanna aoldaite,
ar chodladh go socair i gcuilteanna
de chlúmh lachan,
ar lámhainní de chraiceann éisc.

Ansan d'imís ar bord loinge,
chuireas mo mhíle slán i do choinne.
Chuireas suas le bruíon is le bearradh
ó gach taobh; bhí tráth ann
go bhféadfainn mo chairde a chomhaireamh
ar mhéaranna aon láimhe amháin,
ach ba chuma.

Thugais uait cúrsa an tsaoil
is d'fhillis abhaile.
Tháinig do long i dtír
ar mo leaba.
Chlúdaíos le mil thú
is chonac go raibh do ghruaig
fachta liath is díreach.

Fós i mo chuimhní
tánn tú bachallach,
tá dhá chocán déag i do chúl buí
cas.

My Dearest One

At my life's start you coaxed me
in my youth, through my softness.
You knew well
my head would be turned
by talk of lime-white courts,
of sleeping sound in quilts
of eiderdown,
of fish-skin gloves.

Then you boarded ship
my thousand farewells went with you.
I put up with sarcasm and strife
from every side; there was a time
I could count my friends on fingers
of one hand.
But it didn't matter.

You gave up the world's way
and came back home
your ship docked
on my bed.
I covered you with honey
and saw your hair
was straight and grey.

But still in my memory
you are ringleted:
you have twelve knots
in your curly yellow
locks.

Translated by Michael Hartnett

An Rás

Faoi mar a bheadh leon cuthaigh, nó tarbh fásaigh,
nó ceann de mhuca allta na Fiannaíochta,
nó an gaiscíoch ag léimt faoi dhéin an fhathaigh
faoina chírín singilíneach síoda,
tiomáinim an chairt ar dalladh
trí bhailte beaga lár na hÉireann.
Beirim ar an ghaoth romham
is ní bheireann an ghaoth atá i mo dhiaidh orm.

Mar a bheadh saighead as bogha, piléar as gunna
nó seabhac rua trí scata mionéan lá Márta
scaipim na mílte slí taobh thiar dom.
Tá uimhreacha ar na fógraí bóthair
is ní thuigim an mílte iad nó kiloméadair.
Aonach, Ros Cré, Móinteach Mílic,
n'fheadar ar ghaibheas nó nár ghaibheas tríothu.
Níl iontu faoin am seo ach teorainní luais
is moill ar an mbóthar go dtí tú.

Trí ghleannta sléibhte móinte bogaithe
scinnim ar séirse ón iarthar,
d'aon seáp amháin reatha i do threo
de fháscadh ruthaig i do, chuibhreann.
Deinim ardáin des na hísleáin, ísleáin de na hardáin
talamh bog de thalamh cruaidh is talamh cruaidh de
        thalamh bog—
imíonn gnéithe uile seo na léarscáile as mo chuimhne
ní fhanann ann ach gioscán coscán is drithle soilse.

Chím sa scáthán an ghrian ag buíú is ag deargadh
taobh thiar díom ag íor na spéire.
Tá sí ina meall mór craorac lasrach amháin

The Race

Like a mad lion, like a wild bull,
a wild boar from a Fenian tale,
a hero bounding towards a giant
with a single silken crest,
I blindly drive the car
through the small towns of the west:
I drive the wind before me
and leave the wind behind.

Arrow from bow, bullet from gun.
Sparrow-hawk through flock of small March birds
I scatter miles of road behind.
Figures flash on signposts—
but in kilometres or miles?
Nenagh, Roscrea, Mountmellick
(but have I travelled through these towns?)
mere things that limit speed
mere things that slow me down.

Through geographic barricades
I rush and dart from the west
I gallop towards where you wait
I speed to where you stand.
Heights are hollows, hollows heights
dry land is marsh, marshland is dry,
all contours from the map are gone:
nothing but shriek of brakes and sparks
        of light.

Sun's in the mirror, red and gold
in the sky behind me,
one huge crimson blazing globe—

croí an Ghlas Gaibhneach á chrú trí chriathar.
Braonta fola ag sileadh ón stráinín
mar a bheadh pictiúr den Chroí Ró-Naofa.
Tá gile na trí deirgeacht inti,
is pian ghéar í, is giorrosnaíl.

Deinim iontas des na braonta fola.
Tá uamhan i mo chroí, ach fós táim neafaiseach
faoi mar a fhéach, ní foláir, Codladh Céad Bliain
ar a méir nuair a phrioc fearsaid an turainn í.
Casann sí timpeall is timpeall arís í,
faoi mar a bheadh sí ag siúl i dtaibhreamh.
Nuair a fhéach Deirdre ar fhuil dhearg an laoi
    sa tsneachta
n'fheadar ar thuig sí cérbh é an fiach dubh?

Is nuair is dóigh liom gur chughat a thiomáinim,
a fhir álainn, a chumann na n-árann
is ná coinneoidh ó do leaba an oíche seo mé
ach mílte bóthair is soilse tráchta,
tá do chuid mífhoighne mar chloch mhór
ag titim anuas ón spéir orainn
is cuir leis ár ndrochghiúmar,
ciotarúntacht is meall mór mo chuid uabhair.

Is tá meall mór eile ag teacht anuas orainn
má thagann an tuar faoin taingire
agus is mó go mór é ná meall na gréine
a fhuiligh i mo scáthán anois ó chianaibhín.
Is a mháthair abhalmhór, a phluais na n-iontas
ós chughatsa ar deireadh atá an spin siúil fúinn
an fíor a ndeir siad gur fearr aon bhlaise amháin
    de do phóigín
ná fíon Spáinneach, ná mil Ghréagach, ná beoir
    bhuí Lochlannach?

Glas Gaibhneach's heart milk through a sieve
her drops of blood strained out
like a picture of the Sacred Heart.
Three scarlet brightnesses are there
and pain so sharp, and sob so short.

I stared at the drops of blood
afraid but almost unaware—
like Sleeping Beauty when she gazed
at her thumb pricked by the wheel,
she turned it over, and over once more
as if her actions were unreal
When Deirdre saw blood
        on the snow
did she know the raven's name?

Then I realize I drive towards you
my dearest friend and lovely man
(may nothing keep me from your bed tonight
but miles of road and traffic lights)
and your impatience like a stone
falls upon us from the sky
and adds to our uneasiness
the awkward weight of my hurt pride.

And more great loads will fall on us
if the omen comes to pass
much greater than the great sun's globe
that lately bled into the glass.
And so Great Mother, cave of awe—
since it's towards you we race—
is it the truth? Is your embrace
and kiss more fine
than honey, beer, or Spanish Wine?

Translated by Michael Hartnett

Ag Cothú Linbh

As ceo meala an bhainne
as brothall scamallach maothail
éiríonn an ghrian de dhroim
na maolchnoc
mar ghine óir
le cur i do ghlaic,
a stór.

Ólann tú do shá ó mo chíoch
is titeann siar i do shuan
isteach i dtaibhreamh buan,
tá gáire ar go ghnúis.
Cad tá ag gabháil trí do cheann,
tusa ná fuil
ach le coicíos ann?

An eol duit an lá ón oíche,
go bhfuil mochthráigh mhór
ag fógairt rabharta,
go bhfuil na báid
go doimhin sa bhfarraige
mar a bhfuil éisc is rónta
is míolta móra
ag teacht ar bhois is ar bhais
is ar sheacht maidí rámha orthu,

go bhfuil do bháidín ag snámh
óró sa chuan
leis na lupadáin lapadáin
muranáin maranáin,
í go slim sleamhain
ó thóin go ceann

Feeding a Child

From honey-dew of milking
from cloudy heat of beestings
the sun rises up the back
of bare hills,
a guinea gold
to put in your hand,
my own.

You drink your fill from my breast
and fall back asleep
into a lasting dream
laughter in your face.
What is going through your head
you who are but
a fortnight on earth?

Do you know day from night
that the great early ebb
announces spring tide?
That the boats
are on deep ocean,
where live the seals and fishes
and the great whales,
and are coming hand over hand
each by seven oars manned?

That your small boat swims
óró in the bay
with the flippered peoples
and the small sea-creatures
she slippery-sleek
from stem to bow

ag cur grean na farraige
in uachtar
is cúr na farraige
in íochtar?

Orthu seo uile an bhfuilir
faoi neamhshuim?
is do dhoirne beaga
ag gabháilt ar mo chíoch?

Tánn tú ag gnúsacht le taitneamh,
ag meangadh le míchiall.
Féachaim san aghaidh ort, a linbh,
is n'fheadar an bhfeadaraís
go bhfuil do bhólacht
ag iníor i dtalamh na bhfathach,
ag slad is ag bradaíocht,
is nach fada go gcloisfir
an 'fí-faidh-fó-fum'
ag teacht thar do ghuaille aniar.

Tusa mo mhuicín a chuaigh
ar an margadh,
a d'fhan age baile,
a fuair arán agus im
is ná fuair dada.
Is mór liom de ghreim tú
agus is beag liom de dhá ghreim,
is maith liom do chuid feola
ach ní maith liom do chuid anraith.

Is cé hiad pátrúin bhunaidh
na laoch is na bhfathach
munar thusa is mise?

stirring sea-sand up
sinking sea-foam down?

Of all these things are you
ignorant?
As my breast is explored
by your small hand
you grunt with pleasure
smiling and senseless.
I look into your face, child,
not knowing if you know
your herd of cattle
graze in the land of giants
trespassing and thieving
and that soon you will hear
the fee-fie-fo-fum
sounding in your ear.

You are my piggy
who went to market
who stayed at home
who got bread and butter
who got none.
There's one good bite in you
but hardly two—
I like your flesh
but not the broth thereof.

And who are the original patterns
of the heroes and giants
if not you and I?

Translated by Michael Hartnett

ÁINE NÍ GHLINN

Áine Ní Ghlinn was born in Co. Tipperary in 1955. She took
a degree in Irish at University College Dublin in 1976. A poet,
broadcaster and teacher, her first collection was *An Chéim
Bhriste* (Dublin 1984). A second collection, *Gairdín Pharthais*
was published in 1988.

Athchuairt

Nuair a tháinig na páistí
le bláthanna na huaighe
mheasas gurbh aisteach é ar dtús
tú bheith thar n-ais
ag gliúcaíocht amach orm
ó leac na fuinneoige.

Ach tháinig mé isteach air
diaidh ar ndiaidh is
bhraitheas go mba shuaimhneach
do theacht.

D'fhiafraíos díot ar thaitin
na hathruithe sa chistin leat
nó an raibh an bord níos fearr
taobh thiar den doras.

D'oscail tú do phiotail
is thabharfainn an leabhar
gur dhein tú meangadh gáire
is bhí áthas orm gur tháinig tú
fiú go sealadach.

A Revisiting

When the children came home
with flowers from your grave
I thought it strange at first
to have you back
peering out at me
from the window-sill.

But I got used to it
by degrees, and
felt your coming
was a peaceful one.

I asked you if you liked
the changes in the kitchen
or if the table was better
behind the door.

You opened up your petals
and I could have sworn
you smiled
and I was glad you had come back
even for a while.

Translated by Gabriel Fitzmaurice

An Chéim Bhriste

Cloisim thú agus tú ag teacht aníos an staighre.
Siúlann tú ar an gcéim bhriste. Seachnaíonn gach
éinne í ach siúlann tusa i gcónaí uirthi.

D'fhiafraigh tú díom céard é m'ainm. Bhíomar le
chéile is dúirt tú go raibh súile gorma agam.

Má fheiceann tú solas na gréine ag deireadh an lae is
má mhúsclaíonn sé thú chun filíocht a scríobh . . .
    Sin é m'ainm.

Má thagann tú ar cuairt chugam is má bhíonn 'fhios
agam gur tusa atá ann toisc go gcloisim do choiscéim
    ar an   staighre . . .
    Sin é m'ainm.

Dúirt tú gur thuig tú is go raibh mo shúile gorm.
Shiúil tú arís uirthi is tú ag imeacht ar maidin.

Tagann tú isteach sa seomra is feicim ó do shúile go
raibh tú léi. Ní labhrann tú ná ní fhéachann tú ar mo
shúile. Tá a cumhracht ag sileadh uait.

Tá an chumhracht caol ard dea-dhéanta is tá a gruaig
fada agus casta. Cloisim thú ag insint di go bhfuil a
súile gorm is go bhfuil tú i ngrá léi.

Osclaím an doras agus siúlann tú amach.

The Broken Step

I hear you when you climb the stairs. You walk
on the broken step. Everyone else avoids it, but
you walk on it always.

You asked me what my name was. We were together
and you said my eyes were blue.

If you see sunlight at nightfall and if
it awakens a poem in you ...
    That's my name.

If you visit me and I know it's you
because I hear your footstep on the stair ...
    That's my name.

You said you understood and that my eyes were blue.
You walked again on it when you left this morning.

You come into the room and I see from your eyes that
you were with her. You do not speak nor do you look
into my eyes. Her fragrance flows from you.

The fragrance is slender, tall, well-formed, and her
hair is long and curling. I hear you tell her that her
eyes are blue and that you love her.

I open the door and you walk out.

D'fhéadfá é a mhíniú dhom a dheir tú. Dúnaim
an doras.

Ní shiúlann tú uirthi. Seachnaíonn tú an chéim
bhriste. Ní shiúlann éinne ar an gcéim bhriste.
Déantar í a sheachaint i gcónaí.

Mórtas Cine

Caithfear a admháil
gur doirteadh fuil ár sinsear
gur bádh iad
ina dtonntracha fola féin
gur lig siad scread
is iad ag dul go tóin
gur dhein an scread macalla
a dhein macalla
a dhein macalla
a dhéanann fós macalla
inár gcuisleacha inniu.

Is cé go bhfuil an scread
dár stróiceadh óna chéile
go gcoinnímid beo í
ar eagla go gcreidfí
nárbh fhiú
saothar ár sinsear.

You can explain you tell me. I close
    the door.

You do not walk on it. You avoid the broken step.
No-one walks on the broken step. They avoid it
always.

Translated by Gabriel Fitzmaurice

Racial Pride

It must be admitted
that our ancestors' blood was shed
that they were drowned
in the waves of their own blood
that they cried out
as they were sinking
that their cry echoed
echoed
echoed
and echoes still
in our veins.

And though that cry
is tearing us apart
we keep it alive
lest anyone believe
that our ancestors' labour
was not worthwhile.

Translated by Gabriel Fitzmaurice

CATHAL Ó SEARCAIGH

Cathal Ó Searcaigh was born in the Donegal Gaeltacht in 1956. He studied French, Russian and Irish at the National Institute of Higher Education, Limerick and Celtic Studies at Maynooth College. A poet and broadcaster, his first collection, *Súile Shuibhne* (Dublin 1983), was a Poetry Ireland Choice and his second, *Suibhne*, was published in 1987. His selected poems, *Homecoming/An Bealach 'na Bhaile* (with English Translations), was published in 1993.

Dídean

'Tá stoirm air', a deir tú. 'Stoirm mhillteanach.'
Míshocair, coinníonn tú ag siúl an urláir, síos
agus aníos go truacánta, do shúile impíoch.
Lasmuigh tá an oíche ag séideadh is ag siabadh
timpeall an tí, ag cleataráil ag na fuinneoga,
ag béicíl is ag bagairt trí pholl na heochrach.
'Dhéanfadh sé áit a bhearnú le theacht isteach,'
a deir tú, ag daingniú an dorais le cathaoir uilinne.
Tagann roisteacha fearthainne ag cnagadh
na fuinneoige. De sceit, sciorrann dallóg na cistine
in airde. Creathnaithe, preabann tú as do sheasamh
isteach im ucht, ag cuartú dídine.
Ag breith barróige ort, téann mo lámha i ngreim
i do chneas, ag teannadh is ag teannadh. Teas
le teas, scarran do bheola ag súil le póga
díreach is an stoirm ag teacht tríom ina séideoga.
Splancaim is buaileann caor thine do chneas.

Shelter

'It will storm', you said, 'an awful storm'.
Restless, you pace the floor, up
and down plaintively, your eyes suppliant.
Outside the night blows and drifts
about the house, clattering at the windows,
shouting and threatening through the keyhole.
'It would breach a place to come inside',
you say, jamming the door with an armchair.
Volleys of rain knock on the window.
Suddenly, as if in fright, the kitchen blind
rolls up. Quaking, you spring to my breast
for shelter.
Hugging you, my fingers catch
your skin, squeezing, squeezing.
Heat on heat, your lips part to kiss me
as the storm gusts through me.
I flash and a fireball hits your skin.

Translated by Gabriel Fitzmaurice

Searmanas

Ar altóir na leapa
ceiliúraim do chorpsa anocht, a ghile,
le deasghnátha mo dhúile.
Gach géag ghrástúil, gach géag mhaighdeanúil
sléachtaim rompu go humhal
is le paidreacha na bpóg
altaím go díograiseach
gach féith is gach féitheog
is cór na gcéadfaí go caithréimeach
ag canadh iomann do do shuáilcí
do bhéal, do bholg, do bhrollach—
tríonóid thintrí an tsóláis.
Is de réir mar a théann
an searmanas i ndéine is i ndlúthpháirtíocht
tá mo bhaill bheatha ar crith
ag fanacht le míorúilt mhacnais
is tiocfaidh, tiocfaidh go fras
nuair a bhlaisfead diamhrachtaí do ghnéis—
cailís an mhiangais
tiocfaidh, áthas na n-áthas
ina shacraimint, ina thabhartas,
ina theangacha tine an eolais.
Tiocfaidh
réamhaisnéis na bhflaitheas.

Ceremony

On the altar of the bed
I celebrate your body tonight, my love,
with the rites of my desire.
I humbly kneel before
each graceful limb, each maidenly limb
and with kisses of prayer
I fervently give thanks
for every sinew, every muscle
while triumphantly the senses' choir
is singing hymns to your pleasure
your mouth, your belly, your breast—
the fiery trinity of joy.
And as the ceremony intensifies
in solidarity
my body trembles voluptuously
expecting the miracle
and the chalice of my desire
will overflow
when I taste the mystery of your sex.
It will come, joy of joys,
a sacrament, a gift,
the fiery tongues of knowledge
and I will have
intimations of heaven.

Translated by Gabriel Fitzmaurice

Séasúir

Bailc shamhraidh sna cnoic—
i dtitim throm thréan na fearthainne
cloisim míle bó bainne á mblí.

I mbáine an gheimhridh sna cnoic
bíonn an bunsoip trom le sioc—
as a gcuid siní sileann tost.

Seasons

A summer downpour in the hills—
in the strong heavy fall of rain
I hear a thousand cows being milked.

In the winter whiteness of the hills
heavy are the eaves with frost—
from their teats silence drips.

Translated by Gabriel Fitzmaurice

COLM BREATHNACH

Colm Breathnach was born in Cork in 1961. His poems have appeared in various magazines and journals.

Éanlathas

Agus na laethanta eile sin
—nach raibh de théad cheangail eadrainn
ach eagla agus gá—
a chaitheamar ar an gcaolchuid
idir sliabh agus trá.

thagainn chugat le mála lán
de scéalta anuas ón ard:
aiteann is fraoch agus rás
an damh dá fhiach isteach gan tlás
ag rúchladh leis i gcoinnibh fána
na coin ina dhiaidh cruinn ar a shála
gur fhás ar an damh dhá sciathán
is gur éalaigh uainn ina heala bhán,
mála folamh
lán go béal
d'ardscéalta.

An uair sin chínn na héanlaithe
ag éalú leo ód'shúile
ag triall ar thír thar sliabh do ghualainne.

Birdways

And those other days
—all that held us together
was fear and need—
that we spent in dire straits
between a moor and a beach.

I used to come to you with a bag
full of stories down from the hill;
furze and heather and a race
the stag hunted down without stinting
rushing against the slope
the hounds hard on his heels
till two wings grew on the stag
and he flew from us, a white swan,
an empty bag
full to the mouth
of high-flown tales.

That time I saw the birds
flying from your eyes
heading for a land beyond your shoulder.

Aníos ón gcaoláire
a thagtá led'mhála
lán de fhraoch na mara agus boladh na sáile,
eascanna ag lúbadh i sreanga na heangaí,
báid dá scriosadh ar charraigreacha feannta
is feamainn ag slíocadh gruaig na bhfear mbáite,
an t-uisce ag sciobadh uait síoda na hAráibe
is an taoide ag breith léi bairillí fíona na Spáinne.

Le gach focal ód'bhéal
an uair sin chínn arís ag éalú
éanlaithe, ag eitilt as raon do shúl.

Anseo i lár na má dhúinn
tá fuacht nár bhraitheas riamh ar an ard sin
is nár bhraithis a déarfainn ag bun caoláire.
Tá fáil anseo ar lón go rábach,
ach chímse arís id'shúile scáthmhaire
éin ag éalú fé dhéin malairt muráite.

Up from the inlet
you'd come with your bag
full of the sea's fury and the brine smell,
eels writhing in the cords of the net
boats wrecked on stripping rocks,
and seaweed combing drowned men's locks
the water snatching the Arabian silk
the tide carrying off barrels of Spanish wine.

With each word you spoke
I saw the birds again that time
flying out of range of your eyes.

Here on the wide plain
there's a cold I never felt on my hill
nor you ever felt in the inlet I'd say.
There's food aplenty here for the taking
but I see again in your shy eyes
birds flying toward other skies.

Translated by the author